M. L. Ahern

The Great Revolution

A History of the Rise and Progress of the People's Party in the City of Chicago and

County of Cook

M. L. Ahern

The Great Revolution
A History of the Rise and Progress of the People's Party in the City of Chicago and County of Cook

ISBN/EAN: 9783744766630

Printed in Europe, USA, Canada, Australia, Japan

Cover: Foto ©Suzi / pixelio.de

More available books at **www.hansebooks.com**

THE

GREAT REVOLUTION,

A STORY OF THE

𝕽𝖎𝖘𝖊 𝖆𝖓𝖉 𝕻𝖗𝖔𝖌𝖗𝖊𝖘𝖘 𝖔𝖋 𝖙𝖍𝖊 𝕻𝖊𝖔𝖕𝖑𝖊'𝖘 𝕻𝖆𝖗𝖙𝖞

IN THE CITY OF

CHICAGO AND COUNTY OF COOK,

WITH

SKETCHES OF THE ELECT IN ÒFFICE.

BY M. L. AHERN.

———

CHICAGO:

LAKESIDE PUBLISHING AND PRINTING COMPANY.

1874.

TABLE OF CONTENTS.

PART I.

HISTORY OF THE PEOPLE'S PARTY.

PART II.—CITY OFFICERS.

BOARD OF HEALTH.

POLICE JUSTICES AND CLERK.

COLLECTORS AND ASSESSORS.

COMMON COUNCIL.

PART III.

COUNTY OFFICERS.

MISCELLANEOUS.

COMMON COUNCIL STANDING COMMITTEES.

The following is the disposition of standing committees in the Common Council for 1873-4, as appointed, under the Mayor's bill, by Mayor Colvin :*

FINANCE.— McGrath, Spalding, Lynch, Schaffner, Heath.

RAILROADS.— Lengacher, Richardson, McGrath, Stout, Woodman.

JUDICIARY. — Richardson, Cannon, White, Cullerton, Campbell.

FIRE AND WATER.— Corcoran, Mahr, Foley, Woodman, Stone.

SCHOOLS.— Moore, Reidy, Eckhardt, Lynch, Cleveland.

STREETS AND ALLEYS, S. D.— Schmitz, Stone, Coey Foley, Spalding, Dixon.

STREETS AND ALLEYS, W. D.— McClory, Hildreth, Kehoe, Woodman, Miner, O'Brien, Campbell, Cleveland, Eckhardt.

STREETS AND ALLEYS, N. D.— Lynch, Cannon, Corcoran, Lengacher, Stout.

WHARVES AND PUBLIC GROUNDS. — Cannon, Schmitz, Moore, Jonas, Bailey of the Ninth.

* Under this bill, Mayor Colvin presided over the Council. At the expiration of the measure, Ald. Dixon succeeded to the position.

WHARFING PRIVILEGES. — Kehoe, Cleveland, O'Brien, Warren, Clark.

LOCAL ASSESSMENTS.— Fitzgerald, Moore, Reidy, Hildreth, Murphy.

BRIDEWELL.— White, Heath, Bailey of the Ninth, Spalding, Jonas.

LICENSES.— Brandt, Bailey of the Ninth, Mahr, Reidy, Corcoran.

POLICE. — Schaffner, Richardson, Murphy, Cullerton, Mahr.

GASLIGHTS. — Cullerton, Jonas, Pickering, Schaffner, Miner.

HARBOR AND BRIDGES.— Hildreth, Coey, Sidwell, Lengacher, Bailey of the Ninth.

PRINTING.— Foley, Fitzgerald, McGrath, Murphy, Bailey of the Eighth.

MARKETS.— Stout, O'Brien, Warren, Quirk, Sidwell.

PUBLIC BUILDINGS.— Bailey of the Eighth, Schmitz, Coey, Heath, Brandt.

COUNTY RELATIONS.— Pickering, Hildreth, Dixon, Brand, Bailey of the Ninth.

PART I.

HISTORY OF THE PEOPLE'S PARTY.

THE PEOPLE'S PARTY.

The People's Party was built after a very peculiar fashion. The plans and specifications of the doughty structure were prepared by a party of religious adventurers, known as "The Committee of Seventy"—an organization of gentlemen constructed in the interest of temperance, immediately after the passage of the State Liquor Law. Mr. Joseph Medill filled the important duties of contractor; and Mr. Elmer Washburn—whose acquaintance with durable stone work was never questioned—acted as sub-contractor. Before the building was completed, it is true Mr. Medill departed for Europe; and when it was completed, it is a well-known fact that Mr. Washburn suddenly and mysteriously disappeared; leaving behind Messrs. A. C. Hesing, Daniel O'Hara, H. D. Colvin, and others—who were merely assistants—to enjoy the fruits of their labor. These facts to the contrary notwithstanding, the People's Party is an edifice nobody need feel ashamed of.

Messrs. Hesing, O'Hara and Company have decided that the structure will be far more substantial than its predecessor No pains will be spared to make it

2

what it should be. Among other improvements, it is
said, Mr. O'Hara has brought into requisition an in-
genious device — for these days — whereby the People's
money will be perfectly secure, and can be counted at any
moment without extraordinary public excitement.

———·——

Two errors by the Medillian administration, it may be
said, are chiefly responsible for what is known as the People's Party. This organization, it will be allowed, to-day
holds the balance of power in the great city of Chicago.
How those two errors occurred is best known to the administration during whose reign they were committed.

One error was the importation from Joliet, Ill., of a Superintendent of Police for Chicago. The other error was the
attempt to enforce an oppressive liquor ordinance, suggested by a party of men calling themselves "The Committee of Seventy." There was another error, about which
the daily press has spoken considerably. The *Tribune*, of
December 15, 1873, referring thereto, said:

"The disclosures published elsewhere regarding the defal-
cation of the City Treasurer, Mr. David A. Gage, amply
justify all the charges brought against him by his opponents
in the recent city election. They also justify a change in
the city government. Having supported Mr. Gage in good
faith, and having disbelieved the charges preferred against
him until a few days ago, when we learned the real facts
from one of the bondsmen, we are now free to acknowledge
that the People's Party were right from the beginning, so far
as they made their demand that the city money be counted.

Mr. Gage is a defaulter.   A manful acceptance of all the
consequences of his acts is the best way out of his present
difficulties.   We believe that he has sufficient property to
pay everything he owes to the city in time.   Certainly that,
added to the security of his official bond, is sufficient.
Meanwhile, he has placed the City Government in grave
embarrassments."   *   *   *   *

For the benefit of the reader, it may be stated that the
Chicago *Tribune* was an Opposition paper, and the David
A. Gage, of whom it speaks, City Treasurer, under the Medillian administration.   Full particulars regarding Mr. Gage's
misfortune will be found, hereafter, under the head, "Counting the Money."

As regards Error No. 1 :   The gentleman imported from
Joliet was known as Elmer Washburn.   At whose instance
the Mayor, acting under the Mayor's Bill (passed for the
benefit of cities exceeding 10,000 inhabitants), came to be
convinced that there was not a solitary man in Chicago, fit
to be the Superintendent of Police of the city in which he
lived ; that in fact he must needs go to Joliet after him, is
beyond ordinary comprehension.   Certain it is that Mr.
Washburn, when he made that trip from Joliet to Chicago,
was an ill-fated passenger.   From the moment he made his
first appearance in the habiliments of his office, it was pain-
fully evident that Mr. Washburn, while apparently a very
fine gentleman, had mistaken his vocation.   He did not
seem to comprehend the duty of Superintendent of Police
from the outset, in but very rare instances.   Whether he
was acting under impulse or instruction, his orders touch-

ing police duty form the strangest record this generation
has ever witnessed in this particular line. His order for
twelve hours successive service by the patrolmen, among
other fatal mistakes, made him very unpopular among his
men; and his disposition of the force regarding the detec-
tion of liquor-sellers on Sunday, while unwary travelers were
being sand-bagged with impunity, made him the target of
most extensive abuse. At the approach of the fall elections, the following, in regard to Mr. Washburn, appeared in
a leading journal:

"The leaders of the Republican party in this city have
just awakened to the fact — long ago apparent to the blind-
est — that the association of moral ideas is not as strong as
it formerly was in this city. They look profound astonish-
ment when they get on that subject, and remark, 'We have
been losing votes,' and vainly inquire 'Where is the leak?'

*   *   *   *   *

At last, they think they have found it. It is Superintendent
Washburn."   *   *   *   *

The *Times*, of Wednesday, October 22, 1873, under the
head of "How He Does It," contained the following:

"If anybody anywhere knows of anything that has not
been done — outside of his duty — by a Chicago policeman, and will kindly inform Mr. Washburn what that particular thing is, he will detail some of his force to do it at
once. In this category of things done should be included
everything except the suppression of crime. This, however,
is a department of effort in which our excellent chief has
no ambition. What he is evidently attempting to do, and

which he has attained a most astonishing success in doing,
is doing every possible thing except his duty. So marked
is this line of action on the part of our chief, that it leads
the *Times* to make a suggestion which, it believes, will be
greatly to the benefit of the city, by enabling Chicago to ,
avail itself of the services of a very excellent man. This
suggestion is that, in order to have our police business thoroughly attended to, Mr. Washburn should be made comptroller of the currency, or elected as a Trustee in Hyde
Park. Once in either of these positions, or any similar
one, Mr. Washburn would at once give his whole attention
to the police work of Chicago, from the idiosyncracy in his
nature to do with great vigor that which he is not expected
to do, and which is entirely outside of his official position.
It is true that as such Comptroller, he would pay no attention to the currency, or, if a Trustee of Hyde Park, he would
not have the slightest interest in the doings of that domin-
ion. As a Trustee of Hyde Park, he would esteem it his
especial duty to put down houses of ill-fame, and bunko-
players, just as now; while Chief of the Chicago police, he
feels it to be his duty to regulate affairs over in the State of
Indiana. As Comptroller of the currency, he would at once
institute measures against the ten thousand and odd criminals of Chicago, just as now; while Superintendent of our
police, he employs himself as a boss-tailor by inventing a
new roll for the lappel of a coat, or adds an inch to its tails.
It is quite certain that it is only by some such *ruse* as this
that the public will ever succeed in getting Mr. Washburn to
attend to properly policing the Garden City. Meanwhile,

until something is accomplished, as above suggested, the people will watch with interest the vagaries of the erratic Superintendent. When he has arranged affairs in Indiana to suit his ideas, he will probably look into things in Iowa and Kansas. We may also venture to hint to him that the currency act needs tinkering, and which being altogether out of his line, he will be proportionately anxious to take hold of it. This attended to, the spots on the sun might be looked into, and then he might apply himself to discovering a wash that would take the stripes out of a zebra. Of course, there is no reason why the stripes should be taken out of a zebra, which assurance, it is certain, will awaken all Mr. Washburn's ambition to take them out at once. Meanwhile, the thieves, bunko-players, and the rest of the guild, will have to have their own way until such a time as Mr. Washburn's successor shall be appointed."

The following touching farewell notice, given to the mysteriously disappearing Superintendent by a leading journal, will convey an idea of the popularity of his *régime*:

" Elmer Washburn will leave Chicago in about the same manner that he came, with this exception : Many regretted his coming, and but few will sigh at his departure. Those who have entertained the idea that he contemplated resisting the power of the Mayor's bill, or that he would remain in Chicago after his head was chopped off, would undoubtedly be convinced of their error should they visit his late residence, No. 97 Twenty-Second street. The card, "For Rent," is on the door, and not a sign of Elmer, or any member of his household, can be perceived by the closest scrutiny. In a somewhat mysterious manner, his goods and chattels were carted to the Twenty - Second street depot, where they were deposited in a freight car, of either the Illinois or Michigan Central Railroad, and are, before this time, far away. As a master-stroke of economy, the Superintendent detailed one of the patrolmen from the Second Precinct station, to assist in the removal of his goods. On yesterday, rag-pickers were poking about the yard, No. 97; but they found nothing. Our Superintendent is a careful man, and permits nothing to go to waste. Where he will go when he delivers up his star of authority, no mortal knows, but there is a good army whose prayers, could they be of avail, would certainly place one or two oceans between Elmer and Chicago."

As regards error No. 2 : In the fog succeeding the Great Fire, the organization known as a Committee of Seventy sprung into an active existence. Contemporaneously, a Committee of Safety was working energetically, whose creation was suggested as a matter of vigilance regarding the frequent commission of crime in those days. Those Committees should not be confounded. Among the members of said organization of Seventy were, on the outset, and for some time in fact, several very worthy gentlemen. It was a prominent attraction for a time. It then retired from the public gaze. After an interval, however, what was left of it besought the Mayor to enforce the liquor ordinance, the most objectionable features of which come under the head of " Misdemeanors," in the records of the Common Council. To the prayer of the petitioners,

Mayor Medill finally acceded, and issued an order for the enforcement of the Sunday ordinance. The measure of German-American indignation, at this juncture, was full to over-flowing. A committee of this element of our population, appointed by a mass-meeting, called upon his Honor, the Mayor, and assured him that the law was too stringent; but without avail.

The opposition, while quite universal among the dealers — who considered the order most oppressive — was most spirited from this quarter, as the custom among the German people had become sacred to sit beneath the umbrage of some spreading arbor, of a Sunday, and sip in harmony the flowing nectar. It was a custom those people had transplanted from the Fatherland.

The movement was denounced by the German-American element everywhere, as a blow aimed directly at their liberties guaranteed by the Constitution of the country and the State; in fact, they regarded it as an effort to enthrone detested Know-Nothingism in the midst of American citizens of foreign nativity. Indignation meetings followed in quick succession throughout the entire city. The commingling of the religious element with politics was particularly nauseating, inasmuch as it even foreshadowed to them the possible loss of freedom of conscience.

The first shot fired was heard in the Seventeenth Ward. At this meeting, an invitation to co-operate was extended to all liberal elements of all parties and nationalities prone to combat an attempt to destroy personal liberty. A great

German mass-meeting followed at Aurora Turner Hall, on Milwaukee Avenue. Mr. A. C. Hesing, on this occasion, instructed his hearers that they must assure their fellow citizens that they were for good order every day, as they were.

From this point forward, the Liberal movement steadily advanced. At the meetings in the several wards, delegates were appointed upon whom the Union could implicitly rely. Those gentlemen met in Bismarck Hall, and appointed an Agitation Committee. This Committee prepared an Address, from which the following extracts are selected: "A government that rests on material force alone, and adopts coercive measures to compel the people to follow a certain line of conduct, must always be a tyranny, whatever form it assumes." "The question * * * * is that concerning the renewed attempts to enforce certain laws which, for some time, had been obsolete; and to lend assistance to their sanctioning power by additional legislation, and which, for the sake of brevity, is familiarly styled the Temperance and Sunday Laws."

To the Address were appended resolutions pressing a thorough reform of the Civil Service; advocating economy; urging the establishment of more schools, with competent teachers, as a preventative of crime; denouncing arrests where a summons would answer; placing police duty in its proper channel; recognizing the right of the citizen to pass the Sunday in his own way, provided he did not interfere with the choice of any other person; recommending temperance in all things, and a reasonable regulation of the liquor business, such as the appointment of inspectors, and the fining of dealers in impure stuffs; and demanding that drunkards be held strictly accountable as well for their acts committed while drunk, as for committing the act of getting drunk.

The principles embodied in the foregoing mainly constituted the platform adopted at the great mass-meeting in Kingsbury Hall. Cemented by those principles, the great legion of foreign-born Americans, with a very fair sprinkling of native-born Americans, marched to an overwhelming triumph, under the banner of the People's Party, November 4, 1873.

The enforcement of the obnoxious Sunday ordinance came within the province of the Board of Police and Fire Commissioners; as also did the manner in which Superintendent of Police Washburn would enforce said ordinance.

Particulars concerning the same have been carefully taken from the proceedings of the Board; all of which have been classified under the head, " Medill — Washburn — Sheridan," as those three gentlemen represented the two sides to this matter — in fact, it may be added, the two sides to various other matters. So many changes have taken place in the Board that the writer deemed fit to go as far back as the inauguration of the Fire-proof Ticket. Incidents illustrative of Mr. Washburn's conduct, otherwise, are contained therein.

Mancel Talcott and Jacob Rehm joined Mr. Sheridan as
Police Commissioners with the success of the Fire-proof
Ticket. Talcott's entry was imposing. His brow was fur-
rowed with great thoughts apparently, and his lips were set
expressive of marvelous intention. The advance of Rehm
was much less pretentious. He walked into the Board room
like any ordinary individual, and took his seat beside Mr.
Sheridan without the least suggestion of importance. Mr.
Talcott was elected President of the Board at once. For
some time, all was harmony. The Board of Police, controlling the two great arms of the city government,— the
Police and Fire Departments,— became immediately the
cynosure of the public eye. The necessity of a good Fire
Department was uppermost in the public mind as a natural
result of the experience of the great fire. The skeleton of
perished life and property rose up before all citizens alike,
and pointed to a future when the grim ordeal of October 9,
1871, might easily be repeated. It was the necessity of the
hour, in accordance with the platform of the Fire-proof Party,
that the Board should enforce with rigor every ordinance

enacted by the Council for protection against fire. This the Board scrupulously did.

In the spring of 1872, Mr. Rehm resigning, the Mayor appointed in his place Ernest F. C. Klokke. The Board was now composed of Messrs. Talcott, Sheridan and Klokke. About this juncture, the President of the Board, inflated, it would appear, by complimentary notices from the Press, fell into the error of supposing that Talcott constituted the Board of Police, and that his colleagues were merely spectators, as it were. He would fain be Dictator. Such action on the part of Mr. Talcott necessarily fastened upon him the eye of the Press. Hence he derived great titles : "Grand Sachem," "Papa Talcott," "Mr. Oldtalcott," and so-forth. His reign subsequently was one series of strange movements. When he withdrew from the Board, however, he brought with him the warmest personal friendship of his colleagues.

Upon the inauguration of Mr. Klokke, the first matter of importance that arose was the removal by the Mayor of Superintendent of Police Kennedy. This occurred on July 29, 1872. On August 13, 1872, Elmer Washburn succeeded. Mr. Washburn was not a resident of Chicago; knew nothing of its ways, wicked or otherwise, it appears; could not point out the haunts of her evil-doers; indeed, his only qualification to rule a police force was the result of his experience in Joliet State Penitentiary, attending to convicts. The moment Mr. Kennedy was removed, speculation became rife as to his successor. It was presumed that Mr. Medill, with his great good sense, would select, if not an officer from the police force, at least a man conversant with Chicago criminal life, and the way in which to deal therewith. Mr. Medill pursued exactly the different course, however, and proceeded to Joliet State Prison to find a man competent to act as Superintendent of Police of the great city of Chicago. This may be set down as the first grave mistake of the Medillian administration. The act, it cannot be disputed, caused general mortification among Mr. Medill's warmest friends. What policy actuated the Mayor in his action it is impossible to conceive. It was certainly a most discouraging affair to the police force thus made hopeless of deserved promotion; and the marvel is that it did not totally demoralize them. The consequence hereof would be terrible, at the time, when criminals were flocking in by scores from all parts of the country, and murders were being attempted and committed in almost every district of the city.

The necessities of the hour at this particular period of Chicago's history could not be overlooked. It appeared evident to our best citizens that all must act to protect themselves and their homes from concerted outrage at the hands of cut-throats.

A meeting was held on September 12, 1872, in the Chamber of Commerce, on Market street. The purpose of the convention was the repression of crime which, with the resurrection of the city, had assumed gigantic proportions. Henry Greenebaum presided. Three committees were appointed for the three divisions, and comprised twenty-five leading citizens. On September 30th, another meeting was held, called by the Committee of Seventy, then existing for some time, in the interest of temperance. Police Commissioner Talcott was present, and stated that nine-tenths of the crime was induced by drunkenness, and advocated the enforcement of the law closing saloons on the Sabbath. To reach this result, a Committee of Fifteen was sent to Mayor Medill.

This gentleman told the committee that the movement was rather impracticable; the law could not be enforced. The Mayor's address on this occasion was substantially as follows :

"After referring to the demand that the saloons be closed on Sunday, His Honor inquired if this meant that therein all drinking should be prevented, or that to outward appearances no liquor must be consumed therein. The demand clearly stated was this : that the Mayor is commanded to prevent the masses of the people of Chicago from drinking liquor on Sunday in places licensed to supply them on the other six days of the week. Could this be done with the insignificant police force? It appeared to be thought that the saloons had been recently opened on that day, when, in fact, they had never ceased to furnish liquor on any Sunday since the incorporation of the city, more than thirty years ago. Efforts had been made by preceding Mayors to prevent the practice; but the most that was ever accomplished — and that for a short time only — was to force the keepers to pull down their blinds and shut their front doors while the drinking went on. The hotels closed their bars, and the waiters supplied the guests at their rooms. To this extent he thought

the Sunday ordinance could be enforced, but it was ques-
tionable if any less liquor would be consumed. He was willing to issue an order to the police to close the saloons on
Sunday, but could not give any assurance that drinking
would be stopped. In no city like Chicago, with a mixed
population, had the attempt ever succeeded. His Honor
proceeded into a careful consideration of the matter to
prove the strength of his position. He asked the Committee
how could the police prove that liquor was being drunk on
the premises, with the street door locked and the windows
shaded? Should they be orded to break in the doors and
smash the windows on suspicion? Or should they put on
citizen's clothes, slip around through the alley to the kitchen,
and sneak in, call for liquor, and drink it? Or was it
expected that he himself should do it? It could not be ddne
in Chicago. Again, while the ordinance forbade the saloon
keepers to sell liquor on Sunday, it did not forbid the citizen to buy from him on Sunday and drink. There was no
penalty for purchasing and imbibing, and it was hard to convince the dealers that it was wrong to sell on the first day of
the week, when it was legal for anybody to purchase and
drink it on that day. His Honor very sensibly remarked
that to stop liquor drinking would require the aid of one
teetotaler policeman to be stationed in every saloon, billiard
hall, house of ill-fame and tavern in Chicago — say 3,000 in
all. The tax-fighters made it hard work to support 450
policemen; and most of the force sympathized with the
saloons, and he had no power to discharge them. He had
repeatedly made known to members of the Temperance

Organization that he would revoke any saloon keeper's license who was convicted before a magistrate of selling on Sunday. Any citizen knowing it to be done had the legal right to complain before any Justice of the Peace in Chicago, and make proof and have the keeper fined. His Honor closed his address by saying to the Committee that if their meeting supposed that drinking ought be freely indulged on six days of the week, and could be suppressed on the recurring seventh, they had studied human nature to little purpose, and had their first lessons yet to learn."

On October 8, the committee published a reply, accusing the executive department of the city with cowardice. From the reply the following extract is taken: "All the facts go to show that whenever an honest endeavor has been put forth to enforce the Sunday liquor law, it has been successful. The difficulty lies in this, that the liquor interest in our city is active and united, and exerts a controlling influence in the nominating caucuses and conventions. The result is, we have executive officers chosen by their votes who have not the conscience nor the moral courage to do right, and rather violate their oaths of office than to offend the voting power of the saloons, to which they owe their elections."

The report was signed by C. H. Fowler, Abbott E. Kittridge and Philip Meyers, "by order of the Citizens' Committee."

On October 10, Mayor Medill, in a conversation, claimed that the reply of the Committee was very unfair, and referred to the fact that they were quick at seeing the mote in other people's eyes; they should cast the beam out of their own.

The Washingtonian and Father Matthews' Associations never resorted to the constabulary, to prevent men, by animal process, from drinking, but appealed to the mind and conscience; and their success was wonderful.

On the same day, the Committee had an interview with the Police Commissioners. Talcott favored prohibition. Klokke objected to extreme measures, as unadvisable; considering the enforcement of the ordinance impracticable. Sheridan was not present.

On the same day, Mayor Medill, having evidently weakened, sent the following communication to the Board of Police:

BOARD OF POLICE COMMISSIONERS.

Gentlemen: I was waited upon last week by a committee of clergy and laity, who presented some resolutions adopted by a public meeting, asking that the saloons be closed on Sunday, and the ordinance on that subject be enforced. In the general conversation that followed, I expressed a perfect willingness to undertake to do whatever was practicable in the premises, but also some doubts whether with the small police force at command, liquor-drinking on the first day of the week could be effectually prevented in the city. I asked for the active support and assistance of those whom they represented in making complaints before the magistrates, in helping to procure evidence against those who violate the ordinance. But the proposition was coldly received and cynically disposed of. I was unable to procure any promise of efficient aid, whether moral, religious, legal, or physical;

their business seemed to be censure, but not to encourage
or support the authorities. I observe in the partial report
of the interview by their sub-committee, that they waited on
your Board and obtained more encouragement as to the
practicability of enforcing the ordinance. They say *(extract
from newspaper)*: "On the contrary, the Commissioners and
Superintendent of Police upon whom the Committee also
called the same day, declared themselves ready to enforce
such an order when issued by the Mayor, and they antici-
pated no serious trouble in doing so."

I am happy to learn that you anticipate no difficulty in
stopping liquor-drinking in the saloons on Sunday, if an
order is issued by the Mayor to that effect.

I *therefore* and hereby issue said order, and ask your
Board to enforce Section 4, of Chapter 25, of the City Ordinances, and all other ordinances relating thereto.

JOSEPH MEDILL, Mayor.

It may be well to state that no official information was
given to His Honor as to the attitude of the Board.

On October 25, there was issued, by the Committee of
Seventy, an "Address to the People," in which the closing
of saloons Sundays was advocated. On October 26, the
Mayor received a committee of Germans, who went away
satisfied with his position. On October 28, a portion of the
Committee of Twenty-Five met, and committed itself to the
Sunday law; whereupon Mr. Greenebaum resigned his posi-
tion. Mr. Hesing also abandoned the organization.

The best epitaph that could be written on the tombstone of

the Committee of Sèventy is contained in the following con-
clusion of the *Tribune's* article: "THE COMMITTEE OF SEV-
ENTY SOON ABSORBED THE SMALLER ORGANIZATIONS. IT PUT
A TICKET IN THE FIELD LAST YEAR, BUT ITS FIRST VENTURE IN
POLITICS WAS NOT ENCOURAGING. DURING THE WINTER IT
WAS DORMANT; BUT SOME THREE MONTHS SINCE, IT SMELT
THE BATTLE AFAR OFF, AND CAME OUT OF ITS WINTER'S
QUARTERS. IT PROCEEDED TO ORGANIZE THE RECENT CAM-
PAIGN, IN WHICH IT MET WITH A CRUSHING REVERSE.
HEREAFTER, IT WILL BE REMEMBERED IN THE HISTORY OF
LOCAL POLITICS FOR GOOD INTENTIONS, FOR MISERABLE
INEFFICIENCY AS A POLITICAL ORGANIZATION, AND FOR ITS
FAILURE TO EXECUTE THE DESIGN FOR WHICH IT WAS
ORGANIZED."

The fact was, that the Committee of Seventy made a mistake in going into the political business, and never showed
a more illustrious example than when, in the Grand Pacific,
they constructed that "Law and Order Ticket."

So much for the Committee of Seventy.

On December 2d, 1872, Mr. Talcott resigning, C. A. Reno
was appointed to the Presidency of the Police Board. The
Board was now, Reno, Sheridan and Klokke. On the inauguration of Mr. Reno, it became apparent that the Superintendent of Police was arrogating too much, having issued
various orders without its approval. It was resolved, therefore, that all orders should be submitted before issued.

On January 25, 1873, as an evidence of discontent among
the police, the Board received a communication from the
force, asking to be relieved from the order issued by the

Superintendent, compelling them to trável their beats for twelve successive hours. The order impressed the Board at once as tyrannical in the extreme. They accordingly ordered the Superintendent to conform with the established practice of patrol duty.

Now war was declared. The Superintendent failing to comply, it was evident he was acting under the advice of the Law Department concerning the power conferred by the Mayor's bill, and the Board of Police seized the opportunity to test the question whether they had any power at all. On January 28, 1873, accordingly, the Secretary of the Board was directed to present charges against the Superintendent of Police for neglect of duty, incompetency, disobedience of orders, in the violation of the rules and regulations, by enforcing unauthorized orders, and annulling the orders of the Board. Then Dr. Ward was appointed Acting Superintendent. So here was the spectacle of two Police Superintendents at one and the same time, issuing orders of a contradictory nature to the Police Department.

The second volley in the battle of disputed rights was fired from the Mayor's office January 26, 1873. It was a communication from Mayor Medill to the Police Commissioners, notifying said Board of the removal of Police Commissioners Reno and Klokke. The Board concurred in refusing to recognize the authority of the Mayor in said removal. They also instructed the Acting Superintendent to recognize no other authority than the Board which was elected by the people, and a majority of whom were commissioned by the Governor.

From this date up to February 24, 1873, no business was transacted in the Board rooms.

On this day, Carlile Mason and Levi P. Wright, having been appointed by the Mayor, presented certificates. Police Commissioner Sheridan thereupon arose in the crowded rooms of the Police Board, and, with unruffled precision, read the following protest:

"The Council having confirmed the Mayor's nominees for Police Commissioners, and the Mayor and Comptroller having refused to adjust the claims of persons furnishing supplies to the Police and Fire Departments, as well as the claims of the members of said departments, until such time as some other person more acceptable than Mr. Reno, acting as President of the Board, certifies to the correctness of said claims, it becomes necessary that something be done to relieve from embarrassment all those having just claims against the city. There is no doubt in my mind that the Mayor and Comptroller will recognize Messrs. Mason and Wright as the authorized Commissioners, and that, consequently, the business of the departments may be carried on by them, whatever be the merits of their claims as contestants for the position of Police Commissioners. *I am Police Commissioner*, and cannot, if I would, neglect the duties of my office with impunity. *I must act*, and it becomes my duty to act effectively; and, in order to do so, I am constrained by the action of the Mayor and Comptroller to act with Messrs. Mason and Wright, but I do so only to advance the interests of the city, and maintain the discipline and efficiency of the Police and Fire Departments, and not because

I have any doubt as to the legality of the claims of Reno and Klokke; and consequently I will have to serve under protest until this conflict of authority shall be determined by due process of law. I protest, because I am fully satisfied that Commissioners Reno and Klokke, having been elected by the voters of Cook county to the office of Police Commissioners, and having qualified under that election, were in the lawful exercise of the functions of their office, when the Board suspended from duty Superintendent Washburn for inefficiency, neglect of duty, insubordination, and conduct unbecoming a police officer, and that, consequently they were guilty of no offence for which they could be justly or lawfully removed from office; and because I am also satisfied that the power claimed and attempted to be exercised by the Mayor, under and by virtue of the act known as the ' Mayor's Bill,' is *contrary to the genius of our republican institutions* and the spirit of our Constitution, and, also, that even if the power exists, the arbitrary, unjust, and unnecessary exercise of it would not be sustained or even tolerated by the Courts."

The first matter of importance coming before the new Board was the dismissal of the charges against Washburn, February 26, 1873. On April 7, business commenced with the removal by the Mayor of Sergeants Douglas, Macauley, Rehm, and Bischoff. Their offence consisted in obedience of orders issued by the Board of Police.

Then followed, on April 28, 1873, Order No. 20, as follows:

OFFICE OF THE POLICE DEPARTMENT, }
CHICAGO, April 28, 1873. }

General Order No. 20.

1. The commanding officers of districts and precincts
will require their men to enter frequently on Sunday all
places or rooms on their respective beats where they have
any good reason to suspect that intoxicating drinks are sold,
or that cards or other games of chance are being played, for
the purpose of obtaining evidence, if any exist, of the violation of the provisions of Section 3, Chapter 28, of the Revised Ordinances of 1873.   And complaint shall be entered
in accordance with the provisions of Section 2, General
Order No. 6, 1873.

2. In all cases where violations of the provisions of Section 3, Chapter 28, of the Revised Ordinances of 1873 shall
occur, and it shall be difficult to determine whom to sum-
mon, the officer will demand that the license be shown and
enter complaint against the licensee.   If no license is produced, the officer will demand the name and residence of
the party or parties who are tending the bar, if the same
are unknown to him, and enter complaint against him or
them.   If such party or parties fail or refuse to give their
name or residence, the officer will arrest such party or parties at once, take him or them to the lockup, and enter
complaint for the same offense.

3. In no case named in this order shall doors, windows,
or fastenings be broken or forced to gain admission.

ELMER WASHBURN,
General Superintendent. .

The foregoing was the production, it is supposed, of Mayor Medill, Washburn, and the Law Department. This order Mr. Sheridan opposed in his might. Finding it impossible to convince the Mayor of its unwisdom, the Commissioner entered the following protest : " I protest because I regard the order as *unnecessary, odious, and oppressive* ; because the members of the police force are not vested under the charter with the power or authority to lawfully comply with the order, and if they do comply with it, they will have to do so at their own peril ; because it is to my mind clearly unconstitutional, Section 6, Article 2, of the Constitution being as follows : 'The right of the people to be secure in their persons, houses, papers, and effects against unreasonable searches and seizures shall not be violated.' "

To this iron-clad remonstrance, Messrs. Mason and Wright, on May 9, 1873, after formidable preparation, replied as follows :

" *Resolved*, That the protest entered by one of the Commissioners of this Board in the record of the proceedings of the 28th day of April, 1873, was so entered without being first presented to the Board, and that we disapprove of the language used in said protest, as incendiary in character, as tending to incite the force to disobey the orders of the Board, and unreflecting citizens to resist the police in the discharge of their duties. *It is therefore ordered that hereafter* NO PROTEST shall be entered of record, unless the same be first submitted in writing to and permitted by a majority vote of this Board."

Mr. Sheridan's protest appeared in the public journals first; industrious reporters having adroitly secured it.

Following fast upon the foregoing resolution came the following broadside from Mr. Sheridan :

"I protest against the resolution passed by the Board on Friday, because it conveys the idea that my protest, entered against general order No. 20, was surreptitiously placed on record; whereas, the truth is, the objections therein set forth to said order were frequenfly and urgently pressed by me, to dissuade both Messrs. Mason and Wright from approving the order; failing in which, I told them I could not be a party to what I believed to be an unlawful proceeding, and I should protest against it. To which they replied, 'All right; do so. We would rather you should do so than not.' Next morning, I wrote the protest and handed it to the Secretary. It is, therefore, a willful misstatement of the facts in the case, a malignant perversion of my language, a deliberate attempt to gag the free expression of opinion, and is itself the expression of cringing servility to the will of the master."

On May 13, an order was passed requiring the arrest of parties selling, giving away, or in any manner dealing in any vinous, spirituous, or fermented liquors. Sheridan voted in the negative. On May 15, he entered his protest against the order, as unnecessary, injurious, and a dangerous exercise of power. On July 12, Capt. Hickey, convinced that his head was doomed under the Washburn *régime*, resigned the police force..

July 18, furnished an event that cannot be passed over.

Mr. Sheridan, learning of misconduct on the part of a police officer, took his star away from him. The officer complaining to Washburn, had it restored by the Superintendent. Hereupon, Sheridan summoned the chief into his presence on the day referred to. The conversation upon the subject was pretty bitter, the Commissioner feeling that he was insulted by a subordinate, and the Chief not recognizing superiority. The result of the meeting was that Mr. Washburn siezed an inkstand to hurl at the Commissioner's head. Quick second thought, however, held the Superintendent's arm, and he nervously replaced the missile on the desk.

On July 21, the Commissioner preferred charges against the Superintendent, including the specification "ungentlemanly conduct, and conduct unbecoming a police officer." On July 22, the police officer, who had his star restored, was discharged by the Board, under the evidence.

On July 22, a communication was received by the Board from the Council, requesting an investigation of the facts connected with the charges preferred by the Milwaukee press against Washburn. A store had, it appears, been robbed in Milwaukee, and the thieves were tracked to Chicago, and arrested by Chicago officers. The Milwaukee press charged that Washburn refused to give up the property recovered, unless a reward was forthcoming for the officers who caused the arrest. This charge was denied by Mr. Washburn, and the Common Council subsequently acquitted the chief.

The next matter the public journals were called upon

to chronicle, was a communication from the Mayor, setting forth his desire that the Board make a full statement of the facts in the case between Sheridan and Washburn, and submit in writing.   Hereupon, Messrs. Mason and Wright reported the opinion that it would not be for the best interests of the service to spread on the record; that they believed they had found upon investigation that the provocation given by Mr. Sheridan was so great as to greatly palliate the disrespectful language, if not to justify it.

Up to July 28, 1873, there now seemed to be a lull in matters between the members of the Board, the Mayor, the Police force, and the world at large.   On this day, however, Mr. Sheridan succeeded in introducing the following resolution, which was passed :

"*Be it ordered*, That the practice of sending police officers in citizen's clothes to saloons, for the purpose of inducing the keepers thereof to sell intoxicating drinks to such officers, in violation of law, with the view of prosecuting said saloon keepers, be at once discontinued."

On July 29, 1873, Commissioner Mason, having voted for one measure introduced by Mr. Sheridan, resigned.

He was succeeded by Reuben Cleveland.   The advent of this gentleman was signalized by a message from the Mayor, touching the charges preferred by Commissioner Sheridan against Superintendent of Police Washburn. The communication set forth that his Honor, the Mayor, considered the occurrence as a first offense on both (?) sides, and as a case not calling for extreme measures.

On August 4, nevertheless, Superintendent of Police,

Washburn, apologized to Mr. Sheridan on the ground that few men could be milder under equal provocation. Mr. Sheridan did not apologize, as another man *might*, under the Mayor's decision.

In the foregoing brief recital are contained the leading elements in the grand cause for a change in municipal affairs. While the Press, eager to promote universal harmony, no doubt, generally favored the Medillian administration, yet the people watched their interests keenly, and as certain events in this history plainly indicate, subserved them by the movement of November, 1873. The power of that movement is recognized everywhere as having asserted itself against the sentiments of every American newspaper in the city of Chicago.

COUNTING THE MONEY.

For several weeks previous to the election, whispers were gradually spreading throughout the city, the burden of which was that, if it only could be inspected, the City Treasury was in a very wretched condition ; and that the fact was due to the reckless speculations of the City Treasurer, David A. Gage. This gentleman, being a candidate for re-election, and being considered the heaviest card on the "Law and Order" ticket, it is not at all marvelous that the speakers of the People's Party gave the rumor as thorough ventilation as possible throughout the several wards.

To assist the circulation of said rumors, the *Staats Zeitung* caused to be published in English a great number of circulars, whence the following extracts are taken :

"It has been publicly charged and not denied that Gage has deposited the public moneys with banks upon express agreements, that such banks extend him *credit* to the amount of a certain proportion of such deposits. The name of a bank could be given, which held a note of Gage's for $40,-000, and to which he offered $60,000 city deposits on condition of an extension being granted to him. There is scarcely a doubt that the dealings of *private citizen* D. A. Gage with the banks have been based upon the city funds deposited with them by *City Treasurer* D. A. Gage. And it is next to a certainty that if D. A. Gage should cease to have control over the city deposits, the bank credit extended to him on that account would vanish.

"Thus it will be readily understood why D. A. Gage can afford to shoulder all the expenses of the campaign of his party, and offer *to pay the expenses of the People's Party*, if they should nominate him for City Treasurer and Dan O'Hara for County Treasurer. It is, with him, a matter of life or death. But the weakest minded man must be able to see that, if a candidate spends $25,000 in order to obtain an office with a salary of only $4,000, there must be considerably more in that office than the salary.

"As to the means employed, apart from a direct expenditure of money to buy up votes, the following affidavit of Mr. A. C. Hesing tells the tale:

"A. C. Hesing, being duly sworn, deposeth as follows:

"That on or about Wednesday, the 15th of October, he was invited to see a prominent lawyer in H. H. Honoré's block; that he went and saw that lawyer, and that there and then the proposition was made to him to use his influence to secure the nomination of *David A. Gage* by the People's Party for the office of City Treasurer, and of Daniel *O'Hara* for County Treasurer, in consideration of which said David A. Gage would give to the deponent, A. C. Hesing, *the control, for two years, of one-fifth part of the city deposits;* that said proposition was instantly rejected by said deponent;

that, on the Saturday following, the same prominent lawyer met the deponent, A. C. Hesing, in the sample room of Hermann Fink, in the *Staats Zeitung* building, in company with two other gentlemen, and engaged with them in conversation upon a certain article published in the *Staats Zeitung* under the heading, "A few simple questions." That in the course of such conversation said lawyer remarked that that article need not necessarily prevent the *Staats Zeitung* from yet supporting D. A. Gage; that, after the two gentlemen and said lawyer had left the place, said lawyer returned in a short time, and stated to this deponent that another newspaper had to be "*seen*" first, and that, therefore, if this deponent was willing to make arrangements for the support of D. A. Gage, the consideration would have to be reduced from one-half to one-sixth part of the city deposits; that this deponent again refused the offer. That on Sunday afternoon, when this deponent was stepping into his buggy in front of Greenebaum's bank building, the said lawyer hailed him, and, again commencing to speak about the offer theretofore made by him, remarked that *all the papers had been* "SEEN;" that from and after Monday no line would be written in any of the English dailies against David A. Gage, and that this deponent was foolish not to have accepted the propositions made to him. That then this deponent replied that it was of no use to say any more to him, since he was determined to work with heart and soul for the good cause of the People's Party and for the defeat of a damnably corrupt treasury ring.

"Further deponent sayeth not.   ANTHONY C. HESING.

"Sworn to before me this 1st day of November, 1873.

JULIUS ROSENTHAL, *Notary Public.*"

The opposition observing the immense loss their cause was suffering by reason of the insinuations as to the integrity of the alleged best man on their ticket, Mr. David A. Gage was induced, on October 20, to issue the following:

TO HIS HONOR, THE MAYOR, AND COMMON COUNCIL.

Gentlemen: As there have been various speeches made and rumors afloat detrimental to me as a public officer, I most respectfully ask that your body, through a proper committee, would examine my accounts as City Treasurer, and make an official report of the same.   Most respectfully,

DAVID A. GAGE, *Treasurer.*

The members of the Finance Committee were L. L. Bond, Chairman; Mahlon D. Ogden, J. W. McGenniss, J. H. Mc-Avoy, and Geo. Sherwood. At the investigation of the Committee, the two last named gentlemen were not present.

In obedience to Mr. Gage's request, an official report was made of the Finance Committee, as follows:

CHICAGO, ILL., OCT. 31, 1873.

L. L. BOND, ESQ., CHAIRMAN FINANCE COMMITTEE.

Sir: In the matter of the communication of D. A. Gage, Treasurer, referred to our committee, you are authorized to report that we find the Treasurer's accounts correct, and the cash in hand, so that the city funds are entirely safe, and the special funds in the condition required by law.

MAHLON D. OGDEN.
J. W. McGENNISS.

This report the Opposition used with tremendous ostentation, and with considerable success.   While there were many who regarded the report with grave misapprehensions, — owing to the absence of figures which, it is pretty well established, never lie,— yet, the instrument was a most advantageous missile to hurl at the heads of the People's Party. In their speeches through the city, the Opposition introduced the report at every possible opportunity, as illustrative of the base uses to which the People's party had come at last, in order to achieve the success of their ticket.

Had the " Law and Order " ticket been victorious, there is hardly any room to doubt but that the People's party were capable of some very mean business. In that event, David A. Gage would be our present City Treasurer. Victory perching upon the banners of the People's party, however, the great public obtained admission into the inmost recesses of the treasury, and through the fingers of Daniel O'Hara, had the satisfaction of seeing the money counted.

The first reliable intelligence of Mr. Gage's misfortune — Mayor Colvin having just taken his seat — came, it would appear, through Mr. John A. Rice, one of Mr. Gage's bondsmen. On the morning of December 15, this gentleman approached the Mayor elect, and informed him that David A. Gage was $350,000 (three hundred and fifty thousand dollars) short! and that, in order to make good this amount, Mr. Gage would turn over everything he had. Anxiety being wild upon the topic from the first moment the rumor gained circulation, the daily journals next morning, as might be expected, threw forth columns concerning the startling defalcation. For days afterward, the defalcation was the most prominent subject on everybody's tongue. The

4

exposure shocked the entire community, and perfectly dumbfounded those who had voted for the ticket which, for its success, depended almost solely upon the sterling integrity of David A. Gage.

The first thought, when the terrible indignation of the public had given place to reflection, was, in what manner the gigantic loss could be repaired. Now the public eye was turned upon Mr. Gage's bondsmen. But the bondsmen, it was said, claimed they were not altogether responsible, from the fact that shortly after the Medillian administration went into power, it was discovered that Mr. Gage was then short to the extent of some $200,000, and that the city officials, or some of them, knew it. The bondsmen, it seems, claimed that they should not be held for any deficiency previous to their bond being filed.

Whether the bondsmen presumed too much, nevertheless, was susceptible of a test. The legal advisers of the city, accordingly, filed a præcipe in a plea of debt on December 24, placed damages at $1,000,000, and made the following bondsmen of Mr. Gage parties defendant: David A. Gage, William F. Tucker, Albert Crosby, John B. Sherman, James H. McVicker, Nathaniel P. Wilder, John A. Rice, and George W. Gage.

On December 26, Treasurer O'Hara, pursuant to instructions, wrote the following demand upon the Ex- City Treasurer:

"DAVID A. GAGE, ESQ.,

Sir:— Agreeably to the instructions of the law advisers of the city, and as your successor in office, I am requested to demand of you the deficit of money belonging to the City Treasury, amounting to $507,703.58.

I am very respectfully your obedient servant,

DANIEL O'HARA, *City Treasurer.*"

In the meantime conferences were being held by the bondsmen of Mr. Gage, and his friends. At these meetings various propositions were agitated. The result was that, on December 30, a formal conveyance of a trust deed of Mr. Gage's property was made to Mr. George Taylor. This action served in a measure to allay public excitement, which had waxed the more intense under the pressure of the bank panic, and the condition of the vast army of unemployed in the city.

But there was another matter in connection with the situation of Mr. Gage. It was charged against him that he was guilty of perjury. The following oath, required to be taken by the City Treasurer, formed the basis of the accusation:

"I, D. A. Gage, City Treasurer, being duly sworn upon oath, say that the foregoing statement, so far as I know, or have reason to believe, is a fair, accurate and full statement of the matters to which it relates, and of all moneys in my hands which I, or any one for me, has received since my last official account was rendered; and that I have not directly or indirectly used, loaned, invested or converted to my own use, or suffered any one to use, loan, invest or convert to his or their own use, any of the public moneys receivable or received by me or subject to my warrant or control, and that I have rendered true and full account thereof in my said foregoing statement, and further saith not.

D. A. GAGE.,

Sworn, etc.,   FRANK BARRETT,

Notary Public."

It having been known that if Mr. Gage had committed perjury at all he had committed it repeatedly — for it was required that the oath should be taken every month — it evidently became the duty of the State's Attorney to step in. He did so.

On January 2, 1874, State's Attorney Charles H. Reed sent the following to the City Treasurer:

" DANIEL O'HARA, ESQ., CITY TREASURER.

My Dear Friend:— It is reported that David A. Gage, the late City Treasurer, has failed to pay over to you, as his successor, large sums of money belonging to the city of Chicago. In view of proceedings being about to be instituted against him for such failure to pay over to you said sums of money, I hereby request you to forthwith make a formal written demand on said Gage to pay over to you said sums of money. I desire this to be done by you under and by virtue of Section 16, page 179, of the Statutes of Illinois, Gross' Ed., 1871. Please make the demand in such a manner as that you can testify thereto under oath. The demand should be made by you officially and in person.

Respectfully yours,   CHARLES H. REED."

In compliance with instructions Mr. O'Hara visited Mr. Gage, and Mr. Gage did not turn over as requested.

State's Attorney Reed forthwith proceeded to the work of empaneling a Grand Jury. That body was in existence on January 6.

On January 7 the said Grand Jury indicted David A. Gage for failing to pay over the money entrusted to him, and also for false swearing.

On January 8, Mr. Gage was arraigned in the Criminal Court, and his bail was fixed at $100,000 on the former charge, and $10,000 on the latter.

Subsequently the indictment for false swearing was quashed on technical grounds; and that for failing, etc., was sustained. On this indictment Mr. Gage has obtained a chance of venue to Lake county. The State's Attorney, moreover, succeeded in having the following additional indictment returned, which is still pending:

Of the February term of the Criminal Court of Cook County, in said county and State, in the year of our Lord 1874

The Grand Jurors, chosen, selected, and sworn, in and for the county of Cook, in the State of Illinois, in the name and by the authority of the People of the State of Illinois, upon their oaths present that David A. Gage, late of the county of Cook, on the 6th day of December, in the year of our Lord 1873, in said county of Cook, in the State of Illinois aforesaid, was the Treasurer of the city of Chicago, in said county and State, and that he, the said Gage, had been and was the Treasurer of said city for and during the period of one year and more immediately before and prior to the said 6th day of December; and, that he, the said Gage, as such

Treasurer, during the period aforesaid was required by law, at the end of each and every month to render to the Comptroller of said city an account under the oath of him, the said Gage, as such Treasurer, showing the state of the treasury of said city at the date of each of said accounts, and the balance of money in said treasury at the date of each of said accounts, and a fair, accurate, and full statement of all moneys in the hands of him, the said Gage, as such Treasurer, at the date of each of said accounts; and that he, the said Gage, as such Treasurer, was, during the period aforesaid, at the end of each and every month, and oftener if required, required by law to attach said oath to each of said accounts, and to render, present, and deliver said accounts and oaths thereto attached to the said Comptroller; and that he, the said Gage, as such Treasurer, was required by law to render to said Comptroller at the end of the month of November, in the year last aforesaid, an account under the oath of him, the said Gage, attached to said account, showing the state of the treasury of said city at the date of such account, and the balance of moneys in said treasury at the date of such last-mentioned account, and a fair, accurate, and full statement of all moneys in the hands of him, the said Gage, as such Treasurer, at the date of the said last mentioned account; and that he, the said Gage, by his own fault and neglect, failed to render to said Comptroller the account last aforesaid at the end of the month of November last aforesaid.

And that the said Gage, as such Treasurer, was required by law to render the said last named account afterwards, to-wit, on the 6th day of December last aforesaid; and that he, the said Gage, as such Treasurer, was required by law on the said 6th day of December last aforesaid, to render to the said Comptroller an account under the oath of him, the said Gage, showing the state of the treasury of said city on the 1st day of December in the year last aforesaid, and the balance of moneys in said treasury on the said 1st day of December aforesaid, and a fair, accurate, and full statement of all moneys in the hands of him, the said Gage, as such Treasurer, on the said 1st day of December last aforesaid;

And that the said Gage, as such Treasurer, did, on the said 6th day of December, render, present, and deliver to one Augustus H. Burley, he, the said Burley, being then and there the Comptroller of said city, an account showing the state of the treasury of said city on the 1st day of December aforesaid, and the balance of moneys in said treasury on the said 1st day of December, and a statement of all moneys in the hands of him, said Gage, as such Treasurer, on the said 1st day of December;

And that he, the said Gage, as such Treasurer, in order to render the said last named account under his oath, and in order to verify the same by his oath as he was by law required to do as aforesaid, did on the said 6th day of December last aforesaid, come and appear in his own proper person, in said city of Chicago, and county of Cook, before one Francis M. Barrett, he, the said Barrett, being then and there a Notary Public in said city and county, and then and there, in due form of law, sworn by and before him, the said Barrett, as such Notary Public, and did then and there take his oath before said Barrett as such Notary Public, he, the said Barrett, as such Notary Public, then and there having full and competent power and authority to administer said oath to him, said Gage, as such Treasurer in that behalf: and that he, the said David A. Gage, as such Treasurer, being so sworn as aforesaid, upon his oath as aforesaid, did then and there, to-wit, on the day and year last aforesaid, in the city and county aforesaid, before him, the said Barrett, as such Notary Public, falsely, willfully, unlawfully, and corruptly say, depose, swear, and make oath and affidavit, partly written and partly printed, among other things, in substance and to the effect following, that is to say: that there was on the said 1st day of December in the year last aforesaid, so far as he, said Gage, knew or had reason to believe, a balance of money in the treasury of said city in the sum of and to the amount of $1,118,110.49, and that he, the said Gage, on the first day of December, in the year last aforesaid, so far as he, said Gage knew or had reason to believe had in his hands as such Treasurer, moneys in the sum, and to the amount last aforesaid, which said last named account and said oath and affidavit, said Gage, as such Treasurer, rendered, delivered and presented to said Burley, as such Comptroller, the said oath and affidavit being then and there attached to said account, the said 6th day of December last aforesaid, as by said account, oath and affidavit now on file in the proper office of the Comptroller of said city more fully and at large appears. Whereas, in truth and in fact, as he, the said Gage, as such Treasurer, then and there, to-wit, on the said 6th day of December aforesaid, in the city and county aforesaid, well knew that there was not, and had good reason to believe that there was not, on the said 1st day of December aforesaid, a balance of moneys in said treasury in the sum and to the amount of $1,118,110.49; and whereas, in truth and in fact, he, the said Gage, on said 6th day of December, as said Treasurer, well knew that there was not, and had good reason to believe there was not, in his hands as such Treasurer moneys in the sum and to the amount last aforesaid.

And so the Grand Jury aforesaid, upon their oaths and affirmations aforesaid, do present and say that he, the said David A. Gage, as such Treasurer, well knew and had reason to believe, that the said oath and affidavit were willfully and corruptly false in manner and form aforesaid, and that he, the said David A.. Gage, did commit willful and corrupt perjury in manner and form aforesaid, contrary to the statute, and against the peace and dignity of the people of the State of Illinois.

CHARLES H. REED, State's Attorney.

Indorsed: A true bill,

R. R. CLARK, Foreman of the Grand Jury.

Filed Feb. 10, 1874.   AUSTIN J. DOYLE, Clerk.

The civil and criminal actions are still pending. The financial status of Mr. Gage, as to the City Treasury, may be thus stated.

The deficit in the City Treasury, at the expiration of Mr. Gage's term, amounted to $507,703.58. Of this, in the banks were $147,500, leaving what might be called Gage's personal indebtedness $360,203.58.

In the report given as the work of the Finance Committee, it is observed that the signature of Alderman Sherwood, one of the Committee, is not visible. In justice to Mr. Sherwood, the following is published, being a copy of an interview between that gentleman and a *Tribune* reporter:

"Alderman Sherwood, a member of the Committee, had been called to Minnesota by the death of a sister. On his return, after the election, he was asked to sign the report, but declined because he was not satisfied that all was right. He went into the Treasurer's office, and was shown that the balance corresponded with the amount called for by the Comptroller's books. Mr. Sherwood then asked where the money was, and was given a list of the banks in which it was said to be deposited, as follows: *

Commercial	$ 220,883.34
Union Stock Yards	60,000.00
Third National	133,780.53
Union National	204,113.70
Fourth National	50,000.00
Manufacturers' National	15,000.00
Badger's Bank	7,500.00
Second National	115,000.00
Mechanics'	38,500.00
Cook County	101,113.79
Hibernian	10,000.00
Bank of Chicago	5,000.00
State Savings Institution	122,125.08

November Balance, ... $1,083,016.44

* Mr. Sherwood obtained the foregoing statements some days before election ; but, being called suddenly away, did not have an opportunity to analyze them before his return from Minnesota.

"Mr. Sherwood asked to see the bank books, to compare them with the balances above given. The clerk replied that Mr. Gage had taken the bank books away, and that they had not been written up for several months. He (the clerk) had entered the balances as Mr. Gage gave them to him, and, to the best of his knowledge, the accounts were all straight. The stubs on the check‑book showed that there were but two "live" banks,—that is, banks on which checks were drawn,— the others being accounts that had not been disturbed from the time of the fire until the panic. The September balance sheet showed that the Second National had $100,000 and the Mechanics $35,000, while the November balance showed an increase of $15,000 deposited in the former, and of $3,500 in the latter. With the exception of the two banks that were being constantly checked upon, these were the only changes that had been made in the accounts of other banks since the fire. Such is the report which Mr. Sherwood received from the clerk.

"Mr. Sherwood insisted that the bank books should be exhibited fully written up. Soon after, Mr. Sherwood received a note from Mr. Gage requesting him to call at the Pacific Hotel, as he desired to see him. The result was an interview, during which Mr. Gage acknowledged he was short, and appealed to Mr. Sherwood to give him ten days, and he would come out all right; that if he (Sherwood) had not discovered the real facts, nothing would ever be known about them. Mr. Gage felt keenly the situation in which he was placed. He appealed to Mr. Sherwood's generosity, and his appeal prevailed. Mr. Sherwood did not insist upon examining the bank books, though he now thinks he should have done so. He says he pitied Mr. Gage. He told Mr. Gage it was due to him that he should know the worst, that he understood that Mr. Gage had confessed to Mr. Bond and Mr. Burley, since the election, that the deficit amounted to $250,000. Mr. Gage replied that he was short $300,000.

"The interview closed, Mr. Sherwood retiring with the expectation and belief that Mr. Gage would make up the deficiency before his successor demanded a settlement. This explains why the report of the Finance Committee was never sent to the Council."

While pursuing his investigations, Mr. Sherwood procured from the Treasurer's office a statement which is interesting, as it shows the amount in the hands of the Treasurer each month from October, 1871, to October, 1873, inclusive:

Oct. 17, 1871	$ 645,727.98
Dec. 1, 1871	458,463.86
Jan. 2, 1872	516,666.60
Feb. 1, 1872	690,295,66
March 1, 1872	699,359.38
April 1, 1872	821,522.19
May 1, 1872	898,594.66
June 1, 1872	861,925.00
July 1, 1872	1,082,993.74
August 1, 1872	1,275,952.56
Sept. 2, 1872	1,256,584.21
Oct. 1, 1872	1,164,933.40
Nov. 1, 1872	1,077,975,35
Dec. 2, 1872	1,175,048.99
Jan. 2, 1873	1,110,109.12

Feb. 1, 1873..$ 958,901.51
March 1, 1873 .... 984,326.62
April 1, 1873 .... 889,559.53
May 1, 1873....................................... 1,087,051.45
June 2, 1873 .... 1,016,998.99
July 1, 1873 .... 999,588.48
Aug. 1, 1873 .... 1,288,588.39
Sept. 1, 1873 .... 1,444,909.57
Oct. 1, 1873...................................... 1,425,461.56

There were several good causes, in Mr. Sherwood's opinion, why he should not sign the report — if report it was. As regarded the water fund especially, all the information he could secure from officials could not explain to his satisfaction the remarkable shrinkage. All seemed to agree that this fund was over a million dollars before the fire. This fund was sacred under the charter, and Mr. Sherwood could not but be convinced that it was drawn from when the amount in the hands of the Treasurer on Oct. 17, 1871, was found to be $645,727.98.

Had this special water fund been put into bonds, bearing interest, instead of placing the currency in the hands of the Treasurer for speculation, it is certain that the city would draw the interest, and the principle would have been something over a million, instead of $645,727.98, as reported on Oct. 17, 1871.

In his investigation, Mr. Sherwood ascertained that not one of the special appropriation accounts had been balanced since the fire. Then, too, what purported to be the report of the Finance Committee was singularly irregular, as it was *addressed* to the chairman, L. L. Bond, instead of being signed, as is the custom, by the chairman, who is a member of the committee making the report.

If Mr. Sherwood had signed the report, it was the general impression that the white-washing process as regards the city Treasury would have been complete.

In the defense of Mr. David A. Gage, the able services of Hon. Leonard Swett have been secured. In an interview between this learned gentleman and the writer of this work, the following defense by Mr. Gage was ascertained:

" The defense lies in the fact that Mr. Gage used and loaned the City's funds by authority of the City of Chicago. The charter of 1863 provided that the City Treasurer keep the funds in a place designated by the city; and a penalty of imprisonment in the penitentiary was met if the Treasurer converted, used or loaned such moneys in any manner whatsoever, notwithstanding the specifications of a place, the city *never did* furnish a place ; and the city's safe being so insecure as to require a special guard over night, the habit arose, from necessity, to keep the money in the city banks. Each bank, desiring as much of the money as possible, competition arose, and between the years 1863 and 1869, interest was paid on balances, which was kept as a perquisite of office by the City Treasurer.   As the banks were always considered good,— the fact of loaning being notorious — the city came to desire the interest.   Consequently, in the winter of 1869, a law was passed providing that the City Council might, by ordinance, direct the City Treasurer where to place such public money at such a rate of interest, and

with such security as were prescribed by ordinance. Mr.
Gage was the first Treasurer elected after the passage of this
law, and his firŝt official act consisted of a written communication to the Council in which he asked it to act under this
law, and supervise the loaning of the city money.   With
this communication Mr. Gage sent in his official bond in the
sum of $400,0c0, which was the amount required of his pre-
decessors.   The Council, after mature deliberation, determined that if they should direct where the money should be
placed, and, if placed as directed, should be lost, the City
must lose it.   They therefore determined to exact a bond
from Mr. Gage of $2,500,000, with most approved security;
and this indemnified the city in a larger sum than any money
in Mr. Gage's hands, and to permit him to do what he
pleased with the money.   As Mr. Gage assumed, by this
arrangement, personal risk of losing, the City paid him
$10,000 per annum for his risk.   After two years Mr. Gage
accounted with the city, having made more than $100,000
by loans.   Mr. Gage asked the Council for a relief of res-
ponsibility, and to direct where to place the funds.   The
Council declined, telling him to do as he pleased — still
paying him $10,000.   And now, having invested and loaned
in good faith, Mr. Gage denies criminal liability.   It is not
the case of a public officer using the public funds and
becoming a defaulter, but simply a civil liability upon a loan
by authority of the Council.   At the end of Mr. Gage's
term, every dollar had been loaned — aggregating about
$1,000,000.   It was during the great panic of '73, Mr. Gage
collected about $500,000, and paid over about $150,000 in

the city suspended banks, and about $350,000 in other loans. In this situation Mr. Gage, although his liability to do so was very doubtful, assumed payment of deficiencies, and put nearly $600,000 as assets into the hands of a trustee to cover any deficiency ultimately found in the settlement of his accounts."

HOW IT WAS DONE.

The great meeting in the Seventeenth Ward was recognized as the inauguration of the local political campaign. It was held in Thielman's Theatre, on Clybourne avenue, on the evening of May 14.

The meeting was called to order by Mr. A. Hottinger, who denounced the way in which the municipal government was conducted under the Medillian administration. He said he believed so-called temperance notions, with which the heads of the local rulers seemed to be full, could be eradicated as well as slavery had been. He could see nothing but tyranny in the then city government. The Germans would obey the law, or what was called the law, but would seek their redress with other liberal people at the polls in November.

Messrs. Adolphe Schoeninger and Frick were elected President and Secretary.

The former said the object of the meeting was to organize a movement, regardless of party politics, whereby the liberties of the people could be secured and retained. It appeared to be the aim of the city government to abridge the constitutional rights of citizens and make them subservient to its

5

will. Under its Know-Nothing displeasure the Germans had come more than any other people; but they were determined to assert their manhood, and show the so-called temperance people that they were neither drunkards, serfs nor fools. It was hoped that the German papers could conscientiously unite in its support, and that other people would join in the movement.

Mr. Knoblesdorf said that the Germans had been driven to organize for self - protection by the narrow - minded men who were at the head of municipal affairs, and who were endeavoring to force their own sectarian and Know - Nothing opinions down the public throat. The Germans were determined to stand the oppression no longer. They were about to organize for the preservation of their rights and privileges, gauranteed them by the constitution of the country and the state. He believed the result of the November election in Chicago would be a stern rebuke to the Know-Nothing and so-called temperance element. It would show them that the Germans and people of other nationalities were not Puritanical, but progressive and free in their ideas, and jealous of their political rights.

Messrs. Knoblesdorf, Karls, Schmehl, Lengacher and Lindon were appointed a committee on resolutions.

Mr. A. C. Hesing, having been loudly called for, spoke in favor of any movement which would free the people from the thralldom of narrow views and national prejudices, by which the municipal rulers seemed to be swayed. If such a movement could be organized by Republicans and Democrats anxious to preserve the constitutional liberties of the people, so much the better. The record of the Germans could be pointed to with pride. They were not drunkards because they loved convivial beer. They had shown their patriotism and love of American institutions on many a blood-stained field. But it seemed, from present appearances, that all their present sacrifices only entitled them to be trodden under foot in civil life. Their moral record was clearly shown by the national statistics of crime. Knownothingism was striving to get the upper hand again in this city, but it would be put down as it was before. Native Americans had produced more public men at whom the finger of scorn could be pointed, than foreigners. The speaker instanced the cases of Colfax, Brooks, and Ames. Mr. Hesing concluded by stating that he would vote for any man, be he Republican, Liberal, or Democrat, who would exert himself to keep the personal rights of citizens inviolate.

Mr. H. B. Miller followed by a renunciation of the Republican party.

The Committee on Resolutions then returned resolutions expressive of the sentiment of the meeting. The following is a copy of the resolutions:

Resolved, That the present meeting of German citizens, without distinction of party, declares it to be the duty of every liberal-minded citizen to seek in the impending election to work for the future, and not to fight over the past.

Resolved, That we invite all the liberal elements of all nationalities and all parties to co-operate with us.

Resolved, That, in the contest which has been forced upon

us, not merely the oppressive temperance laws are concerned, but the principle of freedom of conscience, and freedom to conduct business of all kinds.

Resolved, That we invite the citizens of all the wards to organize at once, and that the united organizations unite 'in a central body as quickly as possible.

Resolved, That we are of the opinion that not only all liberal-minded citizens, but also the German newspapers, should take a part in this contest; and we, therefore, request them to unite with us in the approaching election, and that we reject with indignation every attempt to make capital out of this common cause.

To carry out these principles, the following measures were agreed to :

That the representatives of the German press pledge themselves to support effectually the efforts of the liberal-minded citizens, and refrain from all personal attacks upon them.

That, at all future elections, we will give our votes to only those men who can give us satisfactory written guarantees that they will act for the preservation of the personal freedom and rights guaranteed by the constitution of the United States, and that they are in favor of the putting down of the unconstitutional and hostile-to-freedom Temperance and Sunday laws, and of the maintainance and freedom of trade.

That a committee be appointed in each ward to see to the naturalization of all who are entitled to become citizens.

That the citizens of all the wards are invited to elect executive committees, and that they unite to form a central committee.

Then came the great German mass meeting, on the evening of May 20, at Aurora Turner Hall, on Milwaukee avenue.

Ex-Alderman John Buehler was elected Chairman, and Mr. Pfurstenberg acted as Secretary.

The first speaker was Mr. A. C. Hesing. He said that he was greatly pleased that the movement begun on the North Side had spread like wildfire into the rest of the city. His exchanges showed that the movement here met with applause everywhere. They must forget the past, and think only how to succeed in the future. The Germans must assure their fellow-citizens that they were for good order every day, and that they would support only good candidates for every position, and turn out every man from the Council who had anything to do with rings or with pushing on these domiciliary visits of police, etc. The German who went to church Sunday morning and to a lager beer garden in the afternoon had a right to have his opinion respected. They should be careful to nominate men who would not betray them. The ward committees would form a central one, which would issue an address to the public, stating their views, and declaring by the Almighty they would not cease till their objects were attained.

Francis A. Hoffman, Jr., followed. The speaker said that the United States was settled by many nationalities. even before the Constitution was adopted. French, Dutch and English had come here. Afterwards an immense immigra-

tion ensued. So many Germans had come that they pre-
served their own customs and manners, to a great extent.
Then the Know-Nothing movement arose, and those who
belonged to it denied their connection, as Henry Wilson had
done. They must in this movement join all hand in hand,
irrespective of anything but their rights. It was said that
the Supreme Court would sustain the Sunday and temperance laws. That was so; but the Federal Supreme Court
had not decided anything of the kind. Slavery was constitutional, and yet it had been put to death. This was not a
question of beer, it was one of personal rights. Why,
instead of fighting the Germans and their rights, did not the
Puritans reprove their Ben. Butlers? The Germans had
fought bravely for American Union. Never would such a
people be conquered in the present contest. They must
sink Republican and Democrat, Catholic and Protestant,
Free Trader and Protectionist, and go in single-hearted to
their contest for freedom and the right, and the good old
customs of the mother land which they had transplanted to
these American shores.

Mr. Emil Dietzsch followed. He said that Germans and
Irish, they were all Americans. For years the Germans had
stood by the Republican party; now the temperance people
were demanding their pound of flesh.

General Herman Lieb and others closed the meeting with
remarks.

Meetings in the various wards followed fast and numerous,
awakening a perfect storm of feeling.

At a meeting of the Chicago Turngemeinde, held in the

North Side Turner Hall, May 21, the following resolutions were adopted:

"WHEREAS, That element of the nation which is inimical to the foreign-born citizens has got control in Chicago, as well as all over the country; of the legislative branches of government, and through them infringes upon the personal liberty of individuals, prostitutes the basis of a Republican form of government, and attempts to force upon the free and independent citizen the straight-jacket of Puritanical views; and

"WHEREAS, The Turngemeinde of Chicago is in duty bound to take up unanimously the side of reformatory, liberal and Democratic ideas in the political and social life; therefore,

"*Resolved*, That we hail with joy the union of all liberal-minded citizens of Chicago, and that we promise to assist with all our might in the battle against the attempts of the Puritans against personal rights and the freedom of trade.

"*Resolved*, That it advise its members to forget all party differences of the past, and to elect only such men as those whose past life is a guaranty of their coincidence with our views, and that they will honestly fulfill the promises given to us.

"*Resolved*, That, as the joint action of all liberal organizations and societies, without distinction of party or nationality, will give this movement sure victory, the Turngemeinde invites all societies to delegate five members each, for mutual consultation and united action.

"*Resolved,* That it is advisable to secure to the movement general confidence, to request societies to elect only such delegates as are honored in their walks of life, and whom nobody can reproach with studying any special interests.

"*Resolved,* That the Turngemeinde absolutely denies the insinuation that in the coming election the German element intends to force itself to the front; far from it; we think we are able to promise the hearty support and warm appreciation of Germans to all those liberal-minded men, of all nationalities, who will fight with us against falsehood and hypocrisy.

"*Resolved,* That the Turngemeinde offers its hall and building, free of charge, for mass-meetings, committee-meetings, and all purposes that will help the cause.

"*Resolved,* That these resolutions be published in the German and English dailies, and the Scandinavian and Bohemian weeklies."

At this juncture, the movement had attained such formidable proportions that the Chicago *Tribune,* on May 24, published the following head-lines, in very bold type, preceding reports of meetings : " THE GERMANS ; THEY ARE RAPIDLY DRIFTING AWAY FROM THE REPUBLICAN PARTY."

Again, in the same journal of May 29, the following head-lines appeared in bold type : " IT IS SPREADING ; THE NEW DEPARTURE OF THE GERMAN AMERICANS." Eight enthusiastic liberal meetings had been held the evening previous.

At those meetings, in conformity with the programme of "the New Departure," delegates were appointed to meet and select an Agitation Committee.

On the evening of May 29th, these delegates met in
Bismarck Hall, in the Teutonia Building, and appointed the
following Agitation Committee: Frank Schweinfurth, Will-
iam Floth, Clovis Tegtmeyer, C. Niehoff, Dr. Matthei, Max
Eberhardt, Emil Muhlke, R. Thieme, F. A. Hoffman, J.
Schiellinger, R. Michaelis, G. R. Korn, William Schwarz, B.
Eisendrath, Carl Dahinten, Philip Stein, H. Schandlin, W.
Schaeffer, Carl Bluhm, R. Freiberg, A. C. Hesing, R. Chris-
tiansen, J. C. Meyer, Peter Hand, A. Erbe, L. Schwuchow,
F. Sengi, and the editors of the various German papers.

This Agitation Committee went to work at once with
great earnestness. The result of their labors was the following Address and resolutions. Said Address and resolutions were presented, on the evening of June 25, to the
Central Committee, in Bismarck Hall, and were adopted
unanimously:

"If it is in times of great political excitement that every
citizen is called upon to discharge his duties in upholding
and supporting the rights of his fellow-men, the integrity of
the nation, or the public welfare and prosperity, it is also at
such times that, from passion and self-interest, men will
lose sight of the goodness of the cause in which they have
enlisted, that they will endeavor to corrupt the true instincts
of the people, in order to make them subservient to their
own personal ends, to their desire of private gain and self-
aggrandizement. The great conflict that was carried on
between two large and powerful sections of this country,
which resulted in the final triumph of the principle advocating the right of freedom from involuntary servitude and

bondage among men, has also fired the passion and encouraged the love of power and personal gain among our people. We have seen the scandalous transactions of men in high office, we have witnessed the attempt of defrauding the public treasury. Instead of the personal rights of the citizen being respected, and the principles of our fundamental laws being carried out, men seek to control those rights. and use the instrument of government as a means of oppression. Men seem to forget that the first condition of liberty is the establishment of some higher principle than compulsion and fear. A government that rests on material force alone, and adopts coercive measures to compel the people to follow a certain line of conduct, must always be a tyranny, whatever form it assumes.

"The question that seems most deeply to interest the people at the present moment, not only in this community, but in all parts of the country, is that concerning the renewed attempt to enforce certain laws which, for some time, had been obsolete, and to lend assistance to their sanctioning power by additional legislation, and which, for the sake of brevity, we familiarly style the Temperance and Sunday laws.

"That these laws are obnoxious to a large and respectable portion of our people, is not so much owing to the fact that they are intended to wage war against the legitimate customs and habits of a large class of our population, but to the well-founded apprehension that they are calculated to aim a deadly blow against the fundamental rights of American citizenship — the right to be protected in the pursuit of happiness, the acquisition of private property, and the exercise of personal liberty. It is the candid opinion of those who undertake to oppose those laws that, although they pretend to be mere police regulations, for the preservation of the public peace, they are dictated by the spirit of religious sectarianism, which is bent upon subjecting the powers of government and the private conduct of its citizens to a system of religious belief to which a number of our citizens, who by no means form a minority, can, from private convictions, never conform.

"We claim that these rules, by which our own civil conduct is to be regulated, tend toward the establishment of a State religion, and violate, if enforced, without qualification, the fundamental rights reserved to the people by our organic laws.

"We hold that moral principles, which are to shape the conduct of our people, cannot effectually be taught in the form of positive law in the halls of legislation, but in the schools, whether public or private, whether denominational or otherwise, and in the sacred confines of our private homes. We hold that in those countries where public instruction is encouraged, and where all essential facilities are freely given, the commission of crime is far less frequent, immoral practices but few in number, and the tone of public morality the most healthy. We are of opinion that, in order to preserve and maintain the virtue of the people, we have to raise the moral standard of our youth, we have to educate the rising generation up to that standard of public and private virtue which has been the pride of those days, in which the fathers of this country reared this noble fabric of government, whose object is to secure the greatest happiness to the greatest number of its citizens.

"In submitting the subjoined resolutions, adopted by a central committee, regularly chosen, we disclaim any intention of disobeying the laws as long as they exist; we shall use all legal means to alter them, and will be guided in our political conduct hereafter by the platform which we submit. We further disclaim all tendencies towards German Nativism, as sometimes charged against us: A common language and views common to citizens of German descent have necessarily caused us to act in harmony in this case, but speaking also the English language, and in the proud consciousness of being American citizens, always true to our adopted country, we call on citizens of all nationalities, whether born here or in another country, to join us in this movement which, we believe, is a combat for right and liberty.

"*Resolved*, That the civil service of the general, state, and local government has become a mere instrument of partisan tyranny, and personal ambition, and an object of selfish greed. It is a scandal and reproach upon free institutions, and breeds demoralization dangerous to the perpetuity of Republican government. We therefore regard a thorough reform of the civil service as one of the most pressing necessities of the hour; that honesty, capacity and fidelity constitute the only valid claims to public employment; that the offices cease to be a matter of arbitrary favoritism and patronage; and that public stations shall become again posts of honor.

"*Resolved*, That in the present state of the public finances, it is imperatively necessary that our city and county affairs be managed in the most economical manner, and that the public monies be husbanded as carefully and frugally as possible.

"*Resolved*, That education of the youth is the most effective agency for the suppression and prevention of crime, and that the establishment of a sufficient number of well-located schools, and the engagement of a large number of competent teachers is one of the greatest demands of this city, and ought at once to be attended to.

"*Resolved*, That we regard it as an outrage and in conflict with the spirit of the times and our institutions, that a man should, except in cases of breach of the peace, be arrested, in cases where his offence, if any, is punished by law with a fine only. In such cases a mere summons answers every just and lawful purpose. All laws and ordinances in conflict with this resolution ought to be modified in accordance therewith.

"*Resolved*, That the police power of the state, county, or city should under no circumstances be wielded in the interest of only-infractions of society for the single purpose of enforcing their individual views and convictions upon another portion of the community, or in the interest of their individual religious views, or in the interest of exclusive modes in which happiness should be pursued and life enjoyed. Recognizing existing institutions, we assent to the demand that during Sunday all business and amusements should be under such restrictions as will in no manner interfere with or disturb the devotion or worship of any class of society, at the same time denying the right of any portion of the community to determine how their neighbors shall pass their Sunday, meaning hereby to concede just what is demanded in return — that all shall be left free to spend their Sunday as they may see fit, provided, only, that they do not commit a breach of the peace, or interfere with any other person exercising exactly the same right of choice, this right of choice, under the above limitations, being, as we believe, a sacred right guaranteed by the institutions of our country.

"*Resolved*, That the cause of Temperance is deserving of aid and assistance by all good men; intemperance in all things whatsoever ought to be combated with all suitable means. For this reason, we are in favor of encouraging the planting and growing of vineyards in this country, and encouraging the brewing of good beer, ales, etc.; and we also recommend the repeal or reduction of duties upon the import of vinous and malt liquors. There ought also to be appointed by the proper authorities inspectors of all the beverages sold publicly, and those found impure and deteriorated ought to be condemned, and the dealers therein fined.

"*Resolved*, That we recommend the passage of an ordinance prohibiting the granting of licenses for keeping saloons, pawn-broker shops, fruit stands, auction stores, hacks, etc., to persons of bad repute.

"*Resolved*, That we consider it a cardinal principle that a person should be held liable for his own wrong only; and for that reason we consider as unjustifiable the statutory enactment making the owner or landlord of premises responsible for the neglect or misdemeanor of his tenant. And for the same reason we demand that drunkards be held strictly accountable as well for their acts committed while drunk as for committing the act of getting drunk.

"*Resolved*, That we recommend the principles and views above set forth to the candid consideration of any good citizen, and we herewith invite all to join us in our efforts to re-establish and maintain our fundamental rights and liberties as citizens of this glorious Republic, and to oppose every candidate for office who is not in sympathy with the spirit of the foregoing resolutions."

At the same meeting it was agreed, on suggestion of Mr. A. C. Hesing, to hold a mass meeting.

On the evening of July 17, seventeen members of the Committee of Seventy met in the Builders' Exchange, on LaSalle street. The meeting here decided the fight to be a square stand-up one on the "Law and Order" side.

Sunday afternoon, August 31, 1873, several gentlemen met in Greenebaum's bank. Present, among others, B. G. Caulfield, W. J. Onahan, A. C. Hesing, General Leib, Justice Boyden, Peter Hunt, Ed. O'Neil, R. Kenney, J. Bonfield, J. H. McAvoy, M. Evans, John Corcoran, Arno Voss, Ed. Phillips, A. Schœnninger, Jacob Rehm, P. M. Cleary, T. Brennan, George von Hollen.

Arno Voss presided. W. J. Onahan acted as Secretary.

Mr. O'Hara said it made him feel proud that he had been a Democrat from childhood; he had lived a Democrat and hoped to die a Democrat. There was in the present administration a dangerous tendency to despotism, and a display of Puritanism which was simply intolerant. While he favored a proper observance of law, he could not but deprecate extreme measures. Crime nor lawlessness did he favor, but he thought the best interests of society could be consulted by adopting such a course as would harmonize all classes of our people. He did not care to see the doors of saloons thrown wide open on Sundays. This would offend a certain class, and be very illiberal. To compromise, why not cause saloon proprietors to keep closed doors and drawn curtains, place the establishments under police surveillance, and suppress disorderly conduct? The main question to insure success was the selection of good men for city officers.

Mr. B. G. Caulfield followed. He said Mayor Medill was elected irrespective of politics, but had sold out to the Law and Order men. In his administration only a moiety of our population had been regarded. Washburn was nothing but an importation, and had displayed a stubborn and ill-governed disposition. The Police Department had become a tool in his hands to enforce Puritanical ideas.

Mr. A. C. Hesing denounced the city government briskly. As an evidence of the manner in which Washburn was conducting police affairs he instanced the case of Dennis Simmons, one of the best officers on the force, who was discharged on a most frivolous charge.

Messrs. Michael Keeley and Lieb also addressed the meeting.

On the evening of Sept. 3, the German-American Central Committee met at Bismarck Hall.

Mr. A. Schœnninger called the meeting to order. He referred to the meeting in Greenebaum's building, where a committee was appointed to confer with the Committee of Agitation.

Mr. A. C. Hesing said that the committee, appointed by the meeting at Greenebaum's bank, consisted of Americans, Irishmen, and members of all nationalities excepting Germans. It was intended hereby that a coalition should be formed.

On the evening of Sept. 5, a meeting was held in Greenebaum's building. Col. Arno Voss called the meeting to order, and stated it was a continuation of the meeting of the Sunday previous.

Alderman McAvoy, Chairman of the Committee appointed to act in connection with the German organization for the purpose of calling a mass-meeting, reported the names for said committee. It was accepted.

A committee of five was appointed to see that all nationalities were represented in committees.

Pending the Committee's report, Mr. A. C. Hesing, having been called upon, gave the history of the organization known as the German-American club. This body, he said, it was intended, should meet another body constructed by this meeting, to exchange suggestions for a platform. This platform, he hoped, would speak in favor of law and order, of which he was in favor as much as Alderman Woodard, or any other man.

Alderman McGrath returned with additional names for

the Committee of Conference, adding also several for the county.

Mr. Keeley moved that the joint committees be instructed to draw up a platform, representing the wishes of the people, and report the same to a mass-meeting.   The motion prevailed.

On Saturday evening, Sept. 6, the coalition met in Bismark Hall, and received the platform of the preceding June.

On the evening of Sept. 12, the platform of Sept. 26, 1873, was adopted.

The following amendment was adopted, offered by Mr. Rosenthal:

Resolved, That there ought also to be appointed, by the proper authorities, inspectors of all beverages sold publicly, and those found impure and deteriorated ought to be condemned, and dealers therein fined.

The following letter was read, from Henry Greenebaum, Esq.:

You will please excuse me from taking any active part in the deliberations of your committee.   While I have no inclination to figure in politics,— my business duties absorbing my time fully,—candor prompts me to say that I am in sympathy with your movement, and I am of the opinion that a municipal ticket, to be composed of *gentlemen possessing honesty and integrity, as well as broad and practical views,* will be overwhelmingly sustained at the polls.

Respectfully,   HENRY GREENEBAUM.

Mr. Rosenthal presented a resolution which was adopted, making the election of judges independent of party issues.

On the evening of Friday, Sept. 26, 1873, a meeting of the joint committee was held in Bismarck Hall.

Mr. Hesing presented the following call which was unanimously adopted :

TO OUR FELLOW CITIZENS.

" In view of our approaching municipal election and the important issues for the welfare of our city involved therein, we call on all those who look calmly and without prejudice upon the political situation, to unite with us in order to secure a good and economical government for the next municipal term. We call upon those who are in favor of an honest city and county administration; who are opposed to intemperance, and endeavor to advance public morals by moral suasion, and not by prohibitory laws; who are in favor of a quiet Sunday by protecting religious services without resort to a stringent general law; who are opposed to the granting of licenses to people of bad repute ; who are in favor of reforming our police so that the force may be the protectors of life and property, and not the tools of intolerance and bigoted fanaticism ; who are in favor of *law and order*, but are opposed to every faction and every candidate who misapply the term for the purposes of intolerance and tyranny,— we invite all citizens of all nationalities to whatever political party they may have formerly belonged, who adopt the above views, to meet in mass-meeting at Kingsbury Hall, on Saturday, October 4, at eight o'clock p. m., for consultation and joint action in regard to the approaching election."

Now came the great and enthusiastic meeting at Kingsbury Hall, Saturday evening. It was an immense demonstration. Clark street was black with the masses.

Among the many transparencies carried by the multitude were observed the following :

" Who owes the city over $2,000,000 in taxes ? The Law and Order Party."

" Equal rights for cottages and palaces."

" Down with an aristocracy of stock swindlers and grain gamblers."

" If Puritans rule, the country is gone."

" Our capital consists of muscle and strength."

" Protection against crime- and a sledge - hammer police force."

" Who resists the payment of taxes ? The leaders of the Law and Order Party."

" The People's choice is the best."

" Fifteen hundred majority for the Fifteenth Ward."

"Let the light shine on our actions, Sundays not excepted."

" Law and order is our motto, but not by force."

" The People's Party is too glorious not to be this time victorious."

" We favor temperance and toleration in all things."

" The People will reform our politics."

" The Mayor's bill will prove a failure."

"Our Party is the strongest."

"The People will reform our Police Department."

"We are tax-payers, not tax-fighters."

"Send Washburn home to Joliet."

"We will vote for the support of law and order."

"Old Barnacles, take back seats."

"Equal rights to all. Down with fanatics."

"The people have arisen in their might. When the people rise fanaticism trembles."

"The great power for good is by moral suasion, and not by prohibition."

"The duty of the police is to arrest criminals and not innocent men."

"The Nineteenth Ward good for 1,000 majority."

"No more gilt-edged candidates."

"We claim our constitutional rights."

"Good-by, Joe; don't you wish you had joined the People's Party?"

H. B. Miller, Esq., occupied the chair. The gentleman referred to the time after the great fire when all, sharing in a common loss, laid aside political sentiments to elect a worthy administration. Soon after the installation of the new officers, a handful of bigoted and fanatical men commenced to plot to undermine the privileges of a weakened people; to undermine privileges they had been accorded from time immemorial. Against the earnest pleadings and protests of our best citizens, the ear of the Executive was opened to them. A superintendent of police had been imported from Joliet, who knew nothing of us, and under his rule the police force, being subjected to a system of mean espion-

age and other humilities, became demoralized. It was now
proposed to place in the field men of honesty, who would
pay attention to the vital interests of the city. The weapon
to be used was the ballot box.

Mr. B. G. Caulfield followed in an energetic speech.
The following is a brief synopsis:

"It is probable that during the preparations made for the
election there will be various meetings held with the view of
bringing out our best citizens. I am glad to attend the
inaugural meeting of the campaign — a meeting of the free
American citizens of Chicago — that is a meeting irrespective
of all feeling of nationality. I have been requested to be
here to - night as a private citizen to express my views
upon the matters in question. I represent no party, I represent no nationality. I favor the election of men un-
pledged to party, whose character and ability will recommend them. There being no political question before us, I
feel as a private individual that I can express only my own
sentiments, for which you are in no wise responsible. We
have come to consult, and all that any speaker can do is to
present his own views. I shall simply lay down the principles
which I think should govern the campaign. For what I say
I am responsible, and I shall exact from the men for whom
I vote the opinions I express. In the first place I shall
oppose combinations of any nationalities made for the purpose of obtaining control of the city government, and of
any coalition of citizens for the purpose of making proscrip-
tive laws. I believe that our first duty is to our Creator, and
that every man should keep the Sabbath holy ; but I do not

see that this is inconsistent with the proper enjoyment of the day. I would recommend that the meeting appoint a committee, to co-operate with any other citizens' movement, with a view to obtain the very best men for city officers. Now, these are my private views, but I believe they enter into the feelings of the campaign. If they are not adopted by this meeting they will still remain my views.

"We must co-operate with all men who have the good of the city at heart, by putting into the field a ticket for which they need never be ashamed. Let us take no man from whom it would be necessary to exact a pledge, no man who is not fit to be trusted to the utmost with the city's management and money. Let us look around at the financial position of the city and country, and ask if it is a time to bicker about paltry police regulations. All other questions must sink into insignificance beside the question of bread—the question that will come home to the workingmen this winter — and that must be looked after. [Applause.] It may be well for Chicago to let her voice be heard in the councils of the nation, warning the people. The cotton and wheat crops alone cannot be bought by the present amount of circulating medium. We want more money. We do not say that the money is not good, but that we have not enough of it, and we must call upon the government to supply the want. It is true it has been said much of our money is wrapped up in bogus railway operations; but, surrounded as we are, we know not where succor is to come from. We must tell the men who hoard up their greenbacks that they are bringing ruin upon us. I would like to return to specie payment, but we cannot do it yet. We must have more money first.

"There is another question. How are we to pay our taxes, now a hundred per cent. higher than ever before, while we are fifty per cent. less able to pay them than a year ago? Some of the poor have judgments against their property for taxes, and it will be sold. Now, what do you think of men who will prate about what we should drink on Sunday, with such a state of things staring them in the face? I want to see the Sabbath respected, but I want no bigotry in our Sunday laws. I want every drunken man arrested. The proper way to protect Sunday from violation is to punish those who violate it. I know nothing inconsistent with the law of God in listening to music on Sunday or any other day. We have music in our churches to elevate our hearts, and why cannot we have it in our parks and on our prairies? I am not in favor of wholesale liquor selling on Sunday, but I want it done under proper regulations.

"I might talk longer, but there are other speakers here, and they will entertain you better than I can; and all I have to say is, indulge in fraternal charity; abolish all discord and bickerings, and let us unite for a single purpose — that of producing a good government for the rich and poor."

The Chairman then read the following letter from Governor Palmer:

SPRINGFIELD, ILL., Oct. 3, 1873.

GENTLEMEN: Your note inclosing a copy of a series of resolutions adopted by a meeting in Chicago, and in which you invite me to be present at a mass-meeting, to be held on to-morrow evening, favorable to the principles recited in the resolutions, is before me. I have withheld my answer until now, with the hope that I might be able to accept your invitation, but I find that it will be impossible.

It affords me great pleasure to express my full concurrence in what I understand to be the leading ideas of the resolutions : that every person should be free to preserve his own happiness, subject only to such restrictions as will afford protection to the equal rights of all others; that questions like that of the mode of the observance of the Sabbath are beyond the rightful domain of legislation; and that every person should be permitted, without legal hindrance, to decide for himself on that, as on all other days, how he shall employ his time, only that he shall not in any sense invade the liberties of others.

In my judgment the highest earthly authority upon all questions of personal morals is each individual citizen, who has the right, subject to the limitations before mentioned, to decide for himself the extent and nature of his own moral duties. But it is due to my own estimate of the character of the American people that I should say that I do not believe that there is any serious difference among them as to the theory of personal rights, upon which our institutions rest, but the real controversy is as to the practical application of these theories to the government of the great cities, and to the regulation of the conduct and the intercourse of their inhabitants. I have no faith in the ministry of the police officer as an agency for the promotion of morals. Under our system of municipal government the authority of its local magistracy and of its police is practically absolute, and the helpless and feeble are often outraged, and thousands are made criminals by being first treated as outlaws. My best wishes are with every movement which is designed to vindicate the rights of every man who is honest and orderly, and regardful of the rights of others, to do on all days that

which seemeth good in his own eyes, without challenge from
any earthly authority whatever.

I am, very respectfully,   JOHN M. PALMER.

General Hermann Lieb, the Hon. A. C. Hesing, the Hon.
Casper Butz, Committee.

Several speeches followed.

Then, amid unbounded enthusiasm, the platform of the
party was adopted as follows :

"*Resolved*, That, in the present state of the public finances,
it is imperatively necessary that our city and county affairs
be managed in the most economical manner, and the public
monies be husbanded as carefully and frugally as possible,
in order that our increased municipal taxation be reduced to
a just and discriminating government, and the expenditures
be made, not for the benefit of any particular class, but for
the benefit of the entire community.

"*Resolved*, That the education of the youth of our country
is one of the most effective agencies for the suppression and
prevention of crime ; that this object is much better attained
by the instruction of our children in the schools than to
attempt to enforce morality by legislation.

"*Resolved*, That the cause of temperance is deserving of
the aid and assistance of every good man. Intemperance
in all things whatever ought to be combated with all suitable
means. But we hold that the desirable object of temperance
can only be accomplished by elevating the moral standard
of the people through enlightened education, and not by
sumptuary laws or special legislation.

"*Resolved*, That we recognize the pursuit of happiness as

one of the inalienable rights of the citizen, and every one should be left free to exercise his right without let or hindrance, except under such restrictions as are imposed by constitutional law; and while we believe that on Sunday all business and amusements should be restricted as in no measure to interfere with or disturb the devotion or worship of any class of citizens, yet we firmly deny the right of any one or any class of individuals to prescribe how or in what manner Sunday or any day shall be enjoyed by a free people in a free Republic.

"*Resolved*, That we are in favor of the passage of an ordinance prohibiting the granting of licenses to persons of bad repute, for any purpose or purposes whatsoever.

"*Resolved*, That there ought also to be appointed by the proper authorities inspectors of all beverages sold publicly, and those found impure and deteriorated ought to be condemned, and dealers therein fined.

"*Resolved*, That we look with deep regret and apprehension upon the demoralized condition of our Police Department. Instead of serving as a department for the protection of life and property of the people, it has been used as an instrument of oppression in the hands of a class of prejudiced and narrow-minded men, and that we deprecate that the legitimate duties of the police force have been prostituted to gratify the intolerant spirit of a minority faction.

"*Resolved*, That the frequent arbitrary arrest of our citizens, in cases where fines only are imposed for breach of city ordinances, is a gross outrage and a violation of constitutional rights, and should not be tolerated by a free and enlightened people.

"*Resolved*, That we consider it a cardinal principle that a person should be held liable for his own wrong only; and for that reason we consider as unjustifiable the statutory enactment making the owner or landlord of premises which have been rented for lawful pursuits responsible for the neglect or misdemeanor of his tenants, and for the same reason we demand that drunkards be held strictly accountable for their acts committed while drunk.

"*Resolved*, That the principles we represent in our platform and resolutions are conducive to law and order; and while we appeal to the sympathy and support of the community at large, regardless of all party affiliations, to endorse them, and the action that we have deemed proper to take in this municipal contest in opposition to a spirit of intolerance, we pledge ourselves that we shall abide by law and order, and denounce any faction that arrogates to itself that name; and to this end we shall oppose every candidate for office who is not in sympathy with the foregoing resolutions."

Mr. J. K. C. Forrest offered the following as an additional declaration of principles:

"In view of the present demoralized condition of the trade, commerce and industry of the country, the meeting held in the financial and commercial center of the great Northwest resolves:

"1.   That the President be respectfully requested to immediately convene Congress in extra session, for the purpose of considering the advisability of issuing a sufficient amount of legal tender currency, based upon the deposit of national securities, and at such high rates of interest as will attract it again to the Treasury upon the restoration of private and corporate credit. The great want at the present time is currency. It is absurd to ask the people to deposit money in banks which do not pay it out on demand. At the same time such deposit of money merely tends to intensify the existing stringency; it simply enables the banks to save themselves at the expense and to the vital injury of the manufacturing and mercantile community. The legitimate and truly commercial mode of calling out currency from its hiding places is to make it for the interest of holders to part with it.

" 2. Congress should be respectfully asked to repeal the existing national bankrupt act. A person with $10,000 of property other than money can now be compelled to sacrifice it for a debt of $150. At the same time such sacrifice, if general, will depreciate the real and personal property of the country from fifty to seventy-five per cent. This would necessarily entail ruin upon hundreds of thousands of our citizens.

" 3. Congress should replace the notes of national banks which have gone into liquidation with legal-tender money. This would save interest and prevent stringency of currency.

" 4. The city of Chicago should promptly issue a sufficient amount of scrip to keep the mechanics and laborers now engaged in municipal improvements in full work.

" 5. The advertised sale of city lots on which are the houses of our citizens, and on which tax payments have not yet been made, should be postponed until the city scrip to be issued has, to some considerable extent, filled the vacuum caused by the withdrawal of money from circulation.

" With this declaration of principles we submit the cause of
the People's Party to our citizens of all religions and nationalities."

When considerable routine business had been done, vehe-
ment cries brought forth Mr. A. C. Hesing, who spoke as
follows :

" FELLOW CITIZENS: I shall entertain you only for a few
minutes, and 'I will say that I never intended to say a word
here to-night.   But, as I have been called upon several times,
I come forward to give you my sentiments in regard to this
present movement.   We are here to-night for the purpose of
organizing a party which shall bring us law and order in
this city ; which shall respect life and property, and give us a
chance, give the poor a chance — you, the laboring classes
of this community, at least the right to enjoy yourselves
according to the dictation of your consciences.   [Applause.]
Now, gentlemen, I recollect the time in this city, and in
other places, when the people — when these very same newspapers — were very glad to hear occasionally from your humble servant who is now before you.   I recollect the time —
and it is not very long since — when the gentleman whom I
now see here to-night before me, who said to-day : " Who
would have anything to do with that crowd that would
assemble at Kingsbury hall to-night? "— when he begged
me to come to the Thirteenth ward and give him a speech
to help elect General Grant and the Republican ticket.   I
recollect the time when this same abused man who stands
here before you, when a boy, at the age of nineteen, opened
his mouth and lifted his voice for the liberty of an oppressed

race in this country. And to-day I stand here to obtain liberty for the oppressed who are here before me. I recollect
the time when these newspapers called upon Mr. Hesing to
organize war clubs to fill our regiments — to induce men to
leave their families — to induce them to take up their mus-
kets and go to the war, and fight the battles for these nabobs
who now try to oppress us. Where would that glorious banner be which floats over us in this hall if it had not been for
you who rescued it from the hands of those robbers? [Ap-
plause.] They say that "the foreigners want to dictate to
us." These same men were not yet born when I went on
the stump to speak for this great nation, and for American
liberty, and liberty for all. [Applause.] It is more than a
third of a century since I·landed in Baltimore — it is thirty-
four years ago that I set my foot on this soil, and to-day I
am yet called a foreigner by this villainous press of the city
of Chicago. [Unusual applause.] I claim to be an American citizen as much as anyone. And if I were in the City
Council I would not go there to put my books that I printed
into the public schools, as some men who now pray for law
and order do. I have been in these Republican conventions, but I have always opened my mouth in defence of
right and justice as against corruption. There is not a man
in this city who can say to my face that I have ever supported a corrupt man for office — that I have ever raised my
voice for a corrupt man for any position. When my native
American friends had not the courage to put a corrupt aspi-
rant aside, they would generally call upon me and say:
"You have the courage, Hesing, step forward and put him

off;" and I generally stepped forward and put him off the ticket. [Applause.] In 1869, when those same reformers thought that the Germans were getting too much influence, they tried to put them down, and what was the result? That law and order Council of 1869, were indicted. [Cries of "Good!" and great applause.] Now, gentlemen, I have as much interest in the city of Chicago as any other man. I have lived here since 1854. I have my business here, which I have to take care of.

"Gentlemen, these men who have built their churches, not with their own money, but with the money of the poor, pray that they alone may have liberty. They think no one else is entitled to liberty and the pursuit of happiness. I say that God knows he bestowed freedom and the rights of the pursuit of happiness upon every one.

"I tell you now, once for all, that I shall not support any man who can be charged with corruption, or has any of these steals sticking to his fingers. [Applause.] I want an honest administration. I want a just administration. I want an administration that will give us law and order not only on Sunday, but on every day in the week. I am in favor of respecting those who attend church, and I believe that others should be. I think their worship should not be interrupted by any parades on the streets, with music and banners, on Sunday. That is the platform on which I stand, and on which I always stood. I am in favor of nominating a man for the Mayoralty like S. S. Hayes, for instance. A man like Thomas Hoyne — a man like Rountree, if he wants it — representative men, like a hundred others I could name;

but I am not in favor of men who call conventions to have God Almighty represented in the Constitution of this country. I believe that God Almighty is represented in the hearts of those humble men who stand here before me. I believe He has very little to do with men like Colfax or Patterson; I am not in favor of a party of men who will support such men for office.

"I tell you, gentlemen, this is not the first time that the humble classes, the hard-working mechanics and artisans, have had to take the reins in their own hands; and when the Chicago *Journal* says to-night that 'the bummers will meet in Kingsbury hall,' I say it insults the 20,000 ballots here represented. [Applause.] They say we can't win; the 'Law and Order' men must win. I think we are the Law and Order party; and I say it myself, like Mr. Caulfield, that if anyone gets drunk on Sunday, or on any other day, he should be arrested and punished, but I cannot admire or agree with the man who goes to church on Sunday, and prays, and goes the next day on the Board of Trade, and swindles his colleagues there out of so many bushels of grain. [Applause.] I say when a man keeps a disorderly house he should be shut up; but I say, too, that a man should not be sent twice to shut up a small saloon, while no one interferes with a dance-house on Clark street. I believe in dealing justice to every man alike. Let us to-night determine that we will have an orderly city, with no sympathy with criminals, and justice to all. I want the law to take its course in every instance; crime punished according to the law, and no pardons. I want every law executed, not only

7

that against Sunday beer selling. The administration of
this city government has been a curse to us for two years,
and I believe we can elect a man like our old Mayors, who
will execute the laws as they should be. Be united, and we
can elect anything. Let them scold us, call us bummers,
tax-eaters, tax-fighters, and all the names they please. I say
that no man in this house ever fought a tax in his life. You
can name no German in this city that ever refused to pay a
tax. It is these men who preach the gospel, and pray at
their meetings, and cry 'Law and Order' at the corners of
the streets, who jump their taxes, and cheat the city out of
what they owe it. They are not able to pay their taxes,
although they have caused them, and they never will be.

"I have worked hard in this cause, notwithstanding the
'Law and Order' people have said it would be a fizzle, and
said that the people had no confidence in Hesing or O'Hara,
or Herr Von Hara and O'Hesing, as the papers put it. We
have fired the first cannon to-night, and its echoes will ring
throughout the campaign. We have filled two halls, and
5,000 people have stood at the door unable to get in. Does
this look like a fizzle? Does this look as if the people had
no confidence in Hesing and O'Hara? Search the poor
man's heart and show him how he is oppressed, how his
comforts and luxuries are stolen from him, and he will fight
his oppressors. The 'Law and Order' people are your
oppressors. They give you no cheap concerts and lectures
to educate you; they will not even let you go to the Exposition on the day when you can dress up and appear like
them, but they go there whenever they please and make you

and their clerks do their work.   They go there and look at
the machinery and furniture and fabrics you have made at
wages of a dollar and a half a day.   I ask Dr. Kittredge or
Dr. Fowler, who preach morality and try to crowd their
words down our throats, to lay their hands on their hearts
and answer if it is right for them to rob the poor of their
privileges.   I ask them what harm there is if, after you have
been working hard in a dirty, dusty shop all the week, you
go to Lincoln Park on Sunday with your wives and babies to
breathe a little of the fresh air the Lord they pray to has
made?   I ask them what harm it would be for you to hear
music there as they hear it in their churches?   I ask them
what harm there is if, when you return, you take a glass of
lager or wine to refresh you?   You are a pack of slaves if
you suffer laws that prohibit this, and if I have to vote alone
on the 5th of November I shall cast my vote to relieve you
of this oppression they have cast upon you."

The nominating convention met at 205 East Randolph
street, on October 24.

Mr. Greenebaum presided; Mr. T. M. Halpine served as
Secretary; and Mr. J. J. Crowley assisted.

Mr. Greenebaum said :—

"Gentlemen, Delegates: A narrow-minded, uncatholic
religious spirit, originating with over-zealous and irresponsi-
ble persons, has forced an issue of proscription and intolerance upon the community which unfortunately, or fortunately,
perhaps, divides the sovereign voters at the approaching municipal election.   An immense mass meeting of the people,

without distinction of party,· religion or nationality, have delegated you gentlemen to nominate candidates for the various offices to be 'filled at the approaching election, solely upon their personal fitness, their honesty, and ability to serve public interest. It is necessary for me to urge upon you to discharge faithfully the high trust imposed upon you. You will enter upon the work before you as the selected representatives of the great People's Party. In a spirit of harmony and rectitude you will make all personal preferences subservient to the general good, and nominate a ticket that will be overwhelmingly sustained at the polls, and avert the impending danger of placing the control of the city in the hands of speculative office-seekers and bankrupts."

Mr. A. C. Hesing offered the following resolutions, which were adopted :

"That this convention emphatically endorse the platform of principles adopted by the people's mass meeting at Kingsbury Hall, October 4, believing that platform to be a true expression of the fundamental doctrines underlying the structure of a free government, and a legitimate protest against all efforts to make sectarianism and class legislation prevalent in our public affairs.

" That as long as our people, discarding the sub-treasury system, expect that the temporary balances in our city and county treasuries shall draw interest, and so long as it is thereby admitted that such public moneys may be made use of by the banks with whom they are deposited, for all those purposes which they may consider as legitimate ; the risk incurred·thereby on behalf of the tax-payers, and the temptation which treasurers may be led into, are so obvious that the public interests require a strict adherence to the one-term principle in regard to the office of custodian of such public moneys.

"That this convention recommend to the Mayor to be elected the appointment of S. S. Hayes as City Comptroller, since it would be difficult to find, among our citizens, one who, by his wide financial experience, his thorough business capacity, and the sterling integrity of his character, is so well fitted for an office which, in view of the present financial embarrassment, is one of the most important and responsible in our municipal administration."

Mr. F. H. Winston offered the following, which was adopted unanimously:

"*Resolved.* That the representatives of the people of the city of Chicago and of the county of Cook, here assembled, do declare as one of our cardinal principles, for the maintenance of which we pledge ourselves and the candidates for whom we propose to cast our suffrages, that we favor and shall demand and insist upon the most rigid economy, as well as scrupulous honesty, in the expenditure of the public money of the city and county, to the end that the present oppressive and almost unbearable burden of taxation may be lightened, and not increased; and that we demand that all extravagant schemes for public buildings to be erected for the purpose of glorifying architects and enriching contractors shall be at least postponed until demanded by the necessities of the public or to give our laborers necessary employment; and that we pledge our candidates to cheerfully

accept the accommodations now provided for the transaction of public business of the offices to which we propose
to elect them."

A. C. Hesing asked permission to introduce the following
from the Democratic Central Committee :

"We the undersigned, members of the Liberal and Democratic Central and Executive Committees of Cook County,
hereby certify that we have not authorized any person for us
to pledge the support of the party, as a party, to what is
known as the "Grand Pacific Hotel" nominations, or to
any other nominations, made or to be made; and believing
it inexpedient to make any nominations as a party at this
time, we leave to all persons the privilege of supporting such
candidates in this local election as their judgment and consciences may dictate.

"And we may say that we beheld with surprise the announce-
ment in the papers that parts of our committee had participated in, and indorsed, the said Grand Pacific Hotel nominations; and we further say that neither of the three named
persons who pretended to represent the party at the Grand
Pacific Hotel are members of the Liberal and Democratic
Central Committee of Cook county, and consequently have
no authority to pledge the party to any nominations except
as private individuals.   " Ch. Koehler.
                                 " Jacob D. Felthausen,
                                 " Robert Kenney,
                                 " Edward Kehoe,
                                 " Albert Michelson,

    " Democratic Central Committee of Cook County."
"Chicago, Oct. 24. 1873."

The communication was accepted and placed on the records of the convention.

The following nominations were then made :

> For Mayor, H. D. COLVIN.
> For City Treasurer, DANIEL O'HARA.
> For City Collector, GEORGE VON HOLLEN.
> For City Assessor, CHARLES DENNEHY,
> For Superior Court Judge, S. M. MOORE.
> For County Court Judge, M. R. M. WALLACE.
> For County Clerk, HERMANN LEIB.
> For Clerk Criminal Court, AUSTIN J. DOYLE.
> For County Treasurer, H. B. MILLER.

Then followed the nominations of George D. Plant, County Superintendent of Schools; Christian Busse, John Herting, William P. Burdick, Thomas Lonergan, and A. B. Johnson, County Commissioners.

Mr. Mark Sheridan, having been called upon, named as Commissioner, C. A. Reno, for the West Side. This gentleman was nominated.

On Monday, October 28, Egbert Jamieson was selected for City Attorney; and Martin Scully, for Police Clerk.

The disposition of the other offices followed.

HOW THE OPPOSITION WORKED.

When it had definitely been ascertained what the People's Party was, and what policy it would pursue, the cry of the Opposition was, "Anything to beat the Hesing-O'Hara combination." To effect this, one of the strangest fusions was formed that has ever been recorded.

On Saturday, Oct. 18th, 1873, in the Grand Pacific, the fusionists, after great confusion, met and nominated the following gentlemen :

For Mayor, L. L. BOND.

For City Treasurer, DAVID A. GAGE.

For City Collector, A. L. MORRISON.

For City Assessor, W. H. P. GRAY.

For City Attorney, I. N. STILES.

For Police Court Clerk, K. R. MATSON.

For Judge of Superior Court, WM. H. PORTER.

For Judge of County Court, M. R. M. WALLACE.

For County Clerk, J. W. BROCKWAY.

For Clerk of Criminal Court, W. K. SULLIVAN.

For County Treasurer, PHILLIP WADSWORTH.

For Superintendent of Schools, A. G. LANE.

For County Commissioners, Messrs. S. OLIN, A. J. GALLOWAY, WM. M. LAUGHLIN, W. B. BATEHAM, S. W. KINGSLEY.

For Police Commissioner, REUBEN CLEVELAND.

On October 23, at Kingsbury Hall, the Committee of Seventy indorsed the Grand Pacific nominations.*

Prior to the nomination of Bond for Mayor, the following letter and reply were read:

CHICAGO, Oct. 22, 1873.

HON. L. L. BOND:

Dear Sir: You have been requested by a respectable body of citizens to become a candidate for the office of Mayor at the approaching municipal election. The representatives of Law and Order will have a convention tomorrow for the nomination of candidates to be supported by them at that election. The office of Mayor is the most important one to be filled. We wish the best man, regardless of nationality, creed, or party, for the place — one who is in accord with our principles. They demand that there shall be honesty and strict economy in the management of our finances, to the end that all expenditures be limited to the actual needs of the people, and that taxation be lightened as much as possible.

We demand that the laws shall be enforced for the protection of life and property. We claim that the protection of every member of society, regardless of age, sex or condition, in person, property and freedom, is the supreme object and duty of government.

We claim that every person has a right, so far as human law is concerned, to his own opinions, and to act upon them as he shall deem best, and to engage in any lawful traffic, and to all the guaranties which the law affords for its conduct and management.

But upon the question of what kinds and modes of traffic

* Here it may be stated that an error heretofore ascribed the *construction* of the Grand Pacific Ticket to the Committee.

are injurious to the citizen, as promoters of disorder, igno-
rance, pauperism and crime, and consequent unnecessary
taxation, the aggregate will of the people is supreme, and
must be obeyed; and to be specific on this point, we insist
that the saloons shall be closed on Sundays; that the
licenses of those who violate the law shall be revoked; that
the keepers of these establishments be required to give
bonds, as required by law, with good security, for the protection and indemnity of those who suffer from violation of
the law; and that the law be enforced by a faithful and efficient police, to the end that crime may be diminished, and
public order maintained.

We respectfully ask if the principles we have announced
meet with your approval. If they do, we pledge to you
such a support as, we believe, will secure your nomination
and triumphant election, with a result which will give to our
city a character and attitude she is entitled to possess and
to occupy before the world. By order of Committee,

S. B. GOOKINS.

MAYOR BOND'S REPLY.

MAYOR'S OFFICE, CHICAGO, Oct. 22, 1873.

THE HON. S. B. GOOKINS.

Dear Sir : Your letter of to-day is at hand, and in reply
I have to say that if the people assign to me the duties
appertaining to the office of Mayor, I shall earnestly endeavor to have all the financial interests of the city honestly
and economically administered, and to that end will do all
the Mayor can do.

With regard to the other points, I have to say that no
executive officer can stand in any other position than that
contained in the oath of office — "that he will faithfully and
impartially execute *all* of the laws to the extent of his
ability," and in the discharge of his duties protect all citi-

zens in their personal and property rights, and in the prosecution of all lawful business enterprises, regardless of the condition of such persons.

As this is the effect of the oath, and the position of an executive officer, it is apparent that I cannot make an exception of the Sunday law, and this necessarily includes the exercise of all lawful means for its enforcement.

It is my purpose to devote my whole energies, if elected, to secure such a government as will promote the safety, honor and welfare of the whole people, and to maintain the good name and credit of our city. No man can do more than this, and no honorable man can do less.

LESTER L. BOND.

The reading occasioned loud and prolonged applause.

On October 29 Mr. Joseph P. Clarkson was nominated for Judge of the Superior Court, *vice* Judge Porter, who died a short time subsequent to his nomination.

THE OFFICIAL RETURNS.

The People's ticket made a clean sweep. In the County it elected a Judge of the Superior Court; a Judge of the County Court; a Clerk of the County Court; a Clerk of the Criminal Court; a County Treasurer; a Superintendent of Schools; five County Commissioners; a member of the Board of Equalization, and a Police Commissioner. The following are the official returns in totals of votes given in the County of Cook and State of Illinois, at an election held in said County on Tuesday, the 4th day of November, A.D. 1873. The candidates in italics were elected:

JUDGE OF SUPERIOR COURT.— *S. M. Moore.* 32,019 *votes.* Joseph P. Clarkson, 21,167.

JUDGE OF COUNTY COURT. — *M. R. M. Wallace,* 53,417. Placed on both tickets. ·

CLERK OF COUNTY COURT.— *Hermann Lieb,* 31,156. James W. Brockway, 22,046.

CLERK OF CRIMINAL COURT.— *Austin Doyle,* 33,031. W. K. Sullivan, 20,163.

COUNTY TREASURER.— *H. B. Miller,* 31,941. Philip Wadsworth, 21,106.

SUPERINTENDENT OF SCHOOLS. — *George D. Plant,* 31,248. A. G. Lane, 21,839.

COUNTY COMMISSIONERS. — *Christian Busse,* 30,837 *; A. B. Johnson,* 31,846 *; Thomas Lonergan,* 31,976; *Wm. B. Burdick,* 31,629; *John Herting,* 31,784 E. A. Lynn, 20,999; S. W. Kingsley, 21,782; W. B. Bateham, 21,340; Wm. M. Laughlin, 21,557; A. J. Galloway, 21,626.

MEMBERS OF STATE BOARD OF EQUALIZATION. — *S. S. Gardner,* 10,673. R. P. Derrickson, 9,173.

POLICE COMMISSIONERS. — *Chas. A. Reno,* 27,148. R. Cleveland, 18,729.

Messrs. Thomas Cannon and Max Eberhardt were elected as County Justices; but the Governor refused to commission on the ground of the non-existence of any such office.

IN THE CITY. — The ticket carried the Mayor, the City Treasurer, the City Attorney, the City Collector, the City Assessor, the Clerk of the Police Court, and the great majority among the Aldermen.

The following are the official returns:

MAYOR. — *H. D. Colvin,* 28,791. L. L. Bond, 18,540.

CITY TREASURER. — *Daniel O'Hara,* 28,761. D. A. Gage, 18,629.

CITY ATTORNEY. — *Egbert Jamieson,* 28,586. Thomas J. Turner, 18,636.

CITY COLLECTOR. — *George Von Hollen,* 28,590. A. L. Morrison, 18,560.

CITY ASSESSOR. — *Chas. Dennehy,* 28,570. Wm. B. H. Gray, 18,705.

CLERK OF POLICE COURT. — *Martin Scully,* 27,544. K. R. Matson, 19,240.

As to the Aldermen, the following are the official returns :

FIRST WARD.— *Foley*, 501.   Lyons, 478.

SECOND WARD.— *Dixon*, 666.   Reid, 285.

THIRD WARD.—*Fitzgerald*, 1,700.   McGenniss, 984; Thomas, 348.

FOURTH WARD.— *Spalding*, 1,735.   McArthur, 688.

FIFTH WARD.— *Stone*, 1,805.   James, 938.

SIXTH WARD.— *Reidy*, 2,212.,   Tracy, 984 ; Conley, 149.

SEVENTH WARD.— *Cullerton*, 2,204.   Millard, 299.

EIGHTH WARD.—*Hildreth*, 1,687.   Fleming, 848 ; McDonald, 695.

NINTH WARD.—*Bailey*, 1,547.   Powell, 1,422 ; Clark, 510; Ryan, 338.

TENTH WARD.— *Woodman*, 1,384.   Greenebaum, 672 ; Eaton, 206.

ELEVENTH WARD.—*White*, 1,136.   Walsh, 809; Ferguson, 89.

TWELFTH WARD.— *Heath*, 1,543.   Courtney, 585.

THIRTEENTH WARD. — *Campbell*, 1,233.   Sherwood, 853; White, 292.

FOURTEENTH WARD.— *Cleveland*, 1,127.   Turtle, 877.

FIFTEENTH WARD.— *McGrath*, 2,874.   Casselman, 454; Brown, 235.

SIXTEENTH WARD.— *Stout*, 2,162.   Hawkinson, 460.

SEVENTEENTH WARD.—*Lengacher*, 2,454.   Pfolstrom, 211.

EIGHTEENTH WARD.— *Murphy*, 1,007.   Handly, 606 ; Bean, 455 ; Barrett, 96.

NINETEENTH WARD.—*Lynch*, 540.   Greeley, 198.

TWENTIETH WARD.— *Jonas*, 837.   Harvey, 494; Kehoe, 283.

THE SUNDAY QUESTION.

Notwithstanding the fact that the platform adopted at Kingsbury Hall clearly foreshadowed the attitude of the Mayor and Aldermen elected on the People's ticket, the Great Defeated yet awaited, in suspense, any opportunity that might arise to cause the total suppression of the sale of liquor on the Sabbath.

Accordingly, when the temperance fever that had suddenly visited the "praying-women" of Ohio reached Chicago, the advocates of the idea that principally caused their discomfiture and total rout at the polls in November, 1873, favored an organization of "praying women" in Chicago.

Throughout Ohio and other states the bands of "praying women," among other resorts adopted, visited places where liquor was sold, and besought the proprietors to close their institutions. To attempt any such thing in Chicago was utter folly; a few venturesome ladies demonstrated the fact in a very brief time.

A strong organization was, nevertheless, subsequently formed, with the object of causing the closing of saloons on Sunday. To attain this end, it was deemed best to present a petition to the Council, as numerously signed as possible. Armed with this, it was quite absurdly hoped that the "praying women" might move to accede to their request a Council in which the People's Party was represented by a majority of about twenty-five to fifteen.

On Friday, March 13, the first movement of importance was inaugurated, in the Methodist Church block. On this occasion it was resolved, by the votes of about six hundred ladies, to approach the Common Council, assembled in session, and entreat them to pass an ordinance in conformity with their wishes. Several clergymen santioned the proceedings with their presence. On the Sunday following, and preceding the day upon which the visit was to be made, several meetings were held in sympathy with the Sunday saloon closing idea; among others, a meeting in the First Baptist church. Several ministers' meetings followed.

The ladies, thus strengthened in their crusade, met in the Methodist Church block, and appointed a committee to present their petition to the Council. At the session, Rev. Arthur Mitchell presented a resolution, adopted at the ministers' meeting, in earnest support of the ladies.

The resolution was received with enthusiasm.

The ladies forming the delegation to the Council now set out upon their mission. Reaching the Council Chamber, they found a miscellaneous gathering of men and boys attracted by the novel demonstration. There was certainly a rough element in the crowd — partaking considerably of the nature of such assemblages as have been noted wherever in the country the "praying women" have been at work. Whatever of insult that element was guilty of can hardly reflect discredit upon the Board of Aldermen.

After the transaction of some routine business, the petition of the ladies was presented to the Council.

Considerable discussion followed. Finally, Ald. Cullerton moved the passage of the engrossed ordinance, as follows:

AN ORDINANCE amending section one (1), chapter fifty (50), and section three (3), chapter twenty-eight (28), of the revised ordinances.

Be it ordained by the Common Council of the City of Chicago:

SECTION 1. The Mayor is hereby authorized to grant licenses for the sale of spirituous, vinous, and fermented liquors to any person who shall apply to him in writing, upon said person furnishing sufficient evidence to satisfy him that he or she is a person of good character, and upon such person executing to the city of Chicago a bond, with at least two sureties, to be approved by the Mayor, in the penal sum of five hundred dollars ($500), conditioned that the licensed party shall faithfully observe and keep all ordinances now in force, or hereafter to be passed, during the period of such license, and that he will keep closed all doors opening out upon any street from the bar, or room where such liquors are sold, on Sunday, and that all windows opening upon any street from such bar, or room where such liquors are sold, shall be provided with blinds, shutters, or curtains, on Sundays,·so as to obstruct the view from such streets into such rooms, and paying for the use of the city fifty-two dollars ($52) and no other fees. On compliance with these requirements a license shall be issued to the applicant, under the corporate seal, signed by the Mayor, and countersigned by the Clerk, which shall authorize the person or persons therein named to sell, barter, give away, or deliver wines and other liquors, whether vinous, or ardent, or fermented, in quantities less than one gallon, in the place

8

designated in the application; *provided*, all licenses issued in pursuance hereof shall expire on the 1st day of July in each year.

SEC. 2. If any person shall keep a common, ill-governed, or disorderly house, or suffer any person to play any game of chance on his or her premises for money, or any other valuable things, any such person, on conviction, shall be fined in a sum of not less than five dollars ($5) nor more than one hundred dollars ($100).

SEC. 3. Section three (3), chapter twenty-eight (28), and section one (1), of chapter fifty (50), of the revised ordinances of the city of Chicago, are hereby repealed.

SEC. 4. This ordinance shall be in force from and after its passage.

The motion of Ald. Cullerton prevailed by the following vote :

Ayes—Richardson, Foley, Fitzgerald, Schmitz, Reidy, McClowry, Cullerton, M. B. Bailey, Hildreth, O'Brien, T. F. Bailey, White, Eckhardt, Mahr, Stout, Schaffner, Lengacher, Cannon, Murphy, Brand, Lynch, and Corcoran.— 22.

Noes— Warren, Dixon, Coey, Sidwell, Pickering, Stone, Clark, Woodman, Miner, Heath, Moore, Campbell, Quirk, and Cleveland.— 14.

The absent Aldermen were Spalding, Kehoe, McGrath, and Jonas.

The attitude of the Council on this question may be stated as 25 to 15, recording Spalding in the negative, and Mc-Grath, Kehoe, and Jonas in the affirmative.

The ladies now besought Mayor Colvin to exercise his veto privilege. This his Honor refused to do, pledged as he was to execute the wishes of The People who elected him.

Ald. Dixon was elected President of the Council on the same evening.

GAGE NOT GUILTY OF PERJURY.

The last indictment for false swearing against David A. Gage, Ex- City Treasurer, which appears in full under the head " Counting the Money," was quashed by Judge Moore March 26, 1874. But one indictment remains at the present writing, being that for failing to pay over. In reference to this indictment, Mr. Gage obtained a change of venue to Lake County. That he will ever be tried thereunder is quite doubtful, however, as the prospects that the city will, in a short time, recover every cent due it, are very promising. In the event of full satisfaction of the debt, a quite general impression exists that to further prosecute would be to persecute. While anticipating so early a settlement of the whole matter, Mr. Gage's counsel yet believe they have a sufficient defense under the indictment for failing to pay over. The main points in said defense are published heretofore, having been elicited* in an interview with Hon. Leonard Swett, Mr. Gage's counsel.

The Court (Judge Moore), in his opinion quashing the last indictment for false swearing, referred to the affidavit made by Mr. Gage and published heretofore. This affidavit conformed substantially to the provision made by the 35th section of chapter 5 of the city charter. But by an amendment it was provided that the word "unlawfully" should be inserted before the word "use" whenever the same occurred. By section 34 it was provided that the treasurer may be directed or authorized by ordinance or resolution of the Common Council to loan, on deposit, the funds of the city, in the banks thereof. Hence the word "unlawfully" was very necessary, preceding the word "use." Inasmuch as said word "unlawfully" was omitted by Mr. Gage, his affidavit did not comply with the statute, and was therefore a voluntary affidavit. There was also concerned a question as to the time of making the affidavit.

The Court concluded as follows :

"Because the affidavit was not authorized by law; or, rather, because it did not conform to the law, and was therefore unauthorized ; and secondly, because it does not appear that the affidavit was made at or about the end of the month, and because it does not appear that the report and affidavit were required by the Comptroller when made, on the 6th of December, 1873, the indictment must be quashed."

The report of a portion of the Finance Committee, published elsewhere in reference to the Gage matter was not "official." Messrs. McGennis and Ogden signed the report after a comparison of the books of the Comptroller, Collector and Treasurer ; presuming the cash to be safe on the showing. If those gentlemen had visited the banks, they might have been snubbed, as Ald. Bateham of the old Committee had been. Upon his visit, it appears he was informed that if Mr. Gage desired to know how much money he had there, Mr. Gage could ascertain. Again, in calm consideration, there were very few men at that time who had not the strongest confidence in Mr. Gage.

PART II.

CITY OFFICERS.

HARVEY D. COLVIN.

Harvey D. Colvin, Mayor of the city of Chicago, was born in Herkimer, Herkimer county, New York, Dec. 18, 1814. Up to his election on the People's ticket, by a majority of 10,251, Mr. Colvin devoted the greatest energies of an uniformly active life to the building up of the United States Express Company in the West. Of this most flourishing institution Mr. Colvin was the General Agent in Chicago, when called upon to stand at the head of the People's ticket — a selection made only after the most mature deliberation of the leaders.

Mr. Colvin's business life commenced in Little Falls, N. Y., where he was engaged for seventeen years in the manufacture of boots and shoes. He subsequently became connected with the American Express Company in the same locality. Removing thence, he organized, in 1854, the United States Express Company in Chicago, with a capital of about $500,000. The growth of the company under his direction, in those twenty years, has been so marvellous that the amount of capital now invested is $6,000,000.

Among the positions of public trust held by Mr. Colvin, while in Little Falls, were the Overseership of the Poor, the County Superintendency of the Poor, and a Town Supervisorship.

Mayor Colvin assumed the duties of his present office on the first day of December, 1873. His Honor's inaugural Address was read before thirty-nine aldermen, as follows: Richardson, Foley, Warren, Dixon, Coey, Fitzgerald, Sidwell,

Spalding, Pickering, Stone, Schmitz, Reidy, McClory, Cullerton, M. B. Bailey, Hildreth, O'Brien, •T. F. Bailey, Clark, Woodman, White, Miner, Heath, Moore, Campbell, Quirk, Cleveland, Eckhardt, McGrath, Mahr, Stout, Schaffner, Lengacher, Cannon, Murphy, Brandt, Lynch, Corcoran, and Jonas. Alderman Kehoe was absent.

The following extracts are culled from the Address as indicative of the attitude of His Honor upon the several important questions referred to:

"During the last municipal administration the attention of our community has, to a great extent, been diverted from all questions referring to an economical management of the city finances, or even to the protection of life and property, by efforts as fruitless as they were frantic, to enforce certain ordinances in regard to the observation of the first day of the week. It is a well known fact that those ordinances, how much soever they may have been in consonance with the public opinion of a comparatively small and homogeneous population at the time of their enactment, have ceased to be so, since Chicago has, by the harmonious coöperation of citizens belonging to different nationalities, grown from a village to the rank of one of the greatest cities of the world. For a series of years it has been the practice of our municipal administration to treat those ordinances as 'obsolete,' and to refrain from enforcing them. It is not intended to denounce that practice, but merely to state that, within the past year, it has become distasteful to a large portion of the community. In our late election the issue has been fairly and squarely made whether the existing ordinances shall be retained and enforced, or, upon the other hand, either repealed or so modified as to be in consonance with the present state of public opinion in our community. A majority of our people, so overwhelming that it would be preposterous to designate their decision as a snap judgment, or to cavil at its meaning, has decided the question in favor of the latter alternative. It behooves all good citizens who believe the principles of our republican form of government to accept that popular decision, to which, following the advice of my predecessor in office, they have appealed. There is no reason to fear that those who conscientiously believe the existing ordinance upon the subject to be dictated by a spirit of religious intolerance incompatible with the spirit of our age, will, on their own part, defy the spirit of mutual toleration. If the Common Council, in its wisdom, and having undoubtedly full power upon the subject, should determine either to repeal or modify the Sunday prohibitions and Sunday clauses in the license law, or to fully secure the religious exercises of a portion of our citizens from all disturbance, without interfering with the harmless enjoyments of other citizens, it will do more than its duty toward the majority of the people of this city.

"Our police system should be conducted upon the principle of the prevention rather than the punishment of crime. Nor should the city seek to obtain revenue by means of any of the prevalent forms of vice. When it does, it becomes *particeps criminis* in the iniquity it professes to punish or suppress. My nature revolts against this barbarous and brutal practice, not pursued for the purpose of extirpating vice, but with the object of adding a few paltry dollars to the public revenue. It shall never receive my sanction. All that can usefully be accomplished in this direction is the mitigation of the more glaring and demoralizing effects of that which in all ages and among all races has existed as an evil that may be mitigated, or, perhaps, regulated, but which has never yet been exterminated.

"Police officers should be made to understand and feel that laws are enacted as much to protect the unfortunate as to punish the wicked. In no case should a person be inhumanly treated simply because he has been arrested for some petty offense or misdemeanor.

. " I am decidedly opposed to the practice of police officers receiving money, in the shape of rewards for services rendered, from any corporation or individual. Let them look to the city alone for remuneration. Such practice will, sooner or later, end in the force becoming merely the instruments of great corporations or wealthy individuals."

His Honor, having comprehensively referred to the condition of the city's finances, which was not very promising, suggested rigid economy as the only resort in the conclusion of his address, He said :—

" In conclusion, gentlemen, I would add that, in view of the prostrated condition of our city treasury, our fellow-citizens loudly call upon you for economical legislation. At the same time they look to me for a prompt interposition of my veto to any measure of wasteful, excessive, or corrupt expenditure. I hope and trust that neither will fail in the duties of our respective provinces. In the event that we do not, we shall acquit ourselves to our own and the public satisfaction, and receive the regard due to good and faithful servants."

DANIEL O'HARA.

Daniel O'Hara, City Treasurer of Chicago, filled a van-guard position on the People's ticket, having assumed the undertaking of opposing David A. Gage in a contest for the custodianship of the city's money. Successive terms as City Treasurer had made Mr. Gage's name the synonym of the loftiest character of official integrity; and the fact that he had paid into the city's exchequer the interest on city deposits — which his predecessors pocketed — seemed to make his re-election a foregone conclusion. This last contest, too, as subsequent developments proved, was the battle of David A. Gage's life. In its result was staked *everything* that concerned his future welfare, and the standing forever afterwards of his connections both public and private. A situation like this shrank from very few availibilities that could tend in the remotest manner to secure success. Against all of these resources, gathered together at suggestion, the People's Party was intrepid enough to present Daniel O'Hara, backed by a simple record for honesty and capability in the discharge of his official duties.

Daniel O'Hara is of Irish descent, as the name indicates, and carries as much of life's sunlight over to the shady side of fifty, as any of his most genial fellow-countrymen. It is his nature to look at the bright side of the picture; and his chief glory is to observe everybody else doing likewise. This cheerful disposition, maintained under all circum-stances, has, during the quarter of a century Mr. O'Hara has dwelt among us, contributed materially to his uniform success in public life.

There are a great many people whose comfort is much heightened by the conviction that others are suffering; while some people are trudging through a merciless rain-storm, that they are snugly esconced in a pair of blankets. A thought like this to a man of Mr. O'Hara's generous im-pulses, is a source of absolute pain. In a commercial point of view, this peculiarity of disposition very rarely enriches the possessor. Yet it has appeared, through the vagaries of circumstances, that Mr. O'Hara's good deeds have been remembered by at least a portion of the world; for to their influence is accredited a goodly proportion of his own pros-perity.

The early life of Mr. O'Hara was devoted to journalism, a field for which he was peculiarly adapted. Twenty years ago, he served as official reporter for the *Chicago Tribune*, and on two occasions he exhibited an ambition to see, prop-erly represented, the interests of the Western Catholics through the *Detroit Vindicator* and *Western Tablet*, both of which journals he founded, only to witness their failure, after he had severed his connection with them. In 1855, aban-doning journalism, he entered the Recorder's office, and was soon created chief clerk.

In 1859, the Legislature created a new court, built upon the then Court of Common Pleas, and christened it the Superior Court. Provision having been made under the new dispensation for additional judges and clerks, Mr. O'Hara, then chief clerk in the Recorder's office, was placed in the field by the Democratic Convention as a candidate for the clerkship. In the race, he was defeated by a trifling majority. He ran so far ahead of his ticket, however, that he sprung at once into the vanguard of his party, universally recog-nized as one of the strongest lions of the fold. This was Mr. O'Hara's first appearance in the political arena.

In 1863, under the new charter, Mr. O'Hara was a candidate for the clerkship of the Recorder's Court, on the ticket led by Hon. Francis C. Sherman, one of the old field-horses of the Democratic party, and one of Chicago's most illustrious pioneers. The Republican party, at the previous election, elected its ticket by a majority of 4,600. But such was the standing of the men placed on the Democratic ticket, that the party made a clean sweep by a trifling majority. Hon. Evert Van Buren was elected Judge of the Recorder's. Court on the same occasion.

In the spring of 1868, the Democratic Convention nominated Hon. W. K. McAllister for the Judgeship of the Recorder's Court, and Mr. O'Hara for the Clerkship.. This was a very fierce fight; — judge and clerk being both staunch Democrats — and resulted in a magnificent victory..

In 1871, under the new constitution, the Recorder's Court became the Criminal Court. The jurisdiction of the Court was now extended to the county; and the judicature was so altered as to require the Judges of the Superior and Circuit Courts to sit therein in rotation. With this change, Hon. W. K. McAllister became a candidate for the Supreme Bench of the State, and was overwhelmingly elected Associate Justice, which distinguished office he yet fills, to the honor of the great State of Illinois and the satisfaction of the people at large.

Mr. O'Hara's term as Clerk of the Criminal Court expired: in the fall of 1873, when the People's Party placed him in the field as a candidate for the City Treasurership of. Chicago.

Throughout his career, Mr. O'Hara has been a stout Democrat, and will always revere the principles inculcated by Senator Douglas, whom he has esteemed as his political. Gamaliel.

JESSE O. NORTON.

The People's Party increased to a very considerable extent the confidence of the public, by the selection of Jesse O. Norton for the responsible office of Corporation Counsel. The adaptability of Judge Norton for the thorough discharge of the manifold duties of the position was universally recognized at once by Press, Bench and Bar. The local press was singularly united in his favor as Corporation Counsel, and a portion of the outside press took early occasion to extol the appointment. The following extract in reference thereto is taken from a leading journal in Joliet (where Judge Norton passed many of his days):

"The numerous friends of Hon. J. O. Norton, in this Congressional district, were pleased to learn of his appointment as Corporation Counsel of Chicago, with an annual salary of six thousand dollars.

"We regard Mr. Norton as not only one of the ablest, but one of the purest public men of the times. For nearly a quarter of a century he was a resident of this city and filled numerous public offices, including that of County Judge, member of the Constitutional Convention, Judge of Circuit Court, member of Congress from this district three terms, and U. S. Attorney, in all of which positions it was never charged that he neglected a single duty or made use of a cent that he was not justly entitled to. His soul is unstained by Credit Mobilierism or official peculation. He is a man of fine ability, and his decisions while on the bench were characterized for their legal knowledge and adherence to correct principles."

Throughout his entire career, Mr. Norton has uniformly

commanded the unqualified confidence of those who have known him — confidence not alone in his ability as a jurist, but confidence in his sterling integrity. Very few men can point to more flattering testimonials in this behalf. Among his invaluable memories, the movement in 1862 to place him as one of the judges in the Court of Claims, is recalled distinguishedly. On this occasion letters of the strongest character, in his favor, were written to the President by such men as Schuyler Colfax, John Covode, O. H. Browning, Lyman Trumbull, Roscoe Conklin, Thaddeus Stevens, R. E. Fenton, and Erastus Corning. While the matter was pending, however, Mr. Norton withdrew from the field, having been re-elected to a seat in Congress.

During his residence in Joliet, the admirers of our subject first introduced him into the arena of politics — a thoroughly unwilling candidate for the public honors vouchsafed to him at the time, it may be said. ˊ Filled with a laudable ambition to go to Congress before his brother graduates of Williams College, in Massachusetts, it is true Mr. Norton stepped into the ranks of the legal profession, bent upon becoming a Congressman. This was his only political desire. Having once gratified it, he placed his whole soul in the practice of the profession he loves so sincerely.

Jesse O. Norton was born in Bennington, Vermont, and is about fifty-seven years of age. Having graduated quite early in life, in Williams College, Massachusetts, with high honors, he came West and settled in Joliet, Illinois. Here he was admitted to the Bar, and practiced for a period exceeding twenty years.

In 1847, he was elected a member of the Constitutional Convention. While so serving, perhaps his most prominent attitude was taken on the question in reference to the exclusion of negroes from the State. He took a bold stand against the exclusion idea; contending that it was entirely unconstitutional. The arguments on which he based his position were conceded, on all hands, to be unanswerable.

In 1850, he was elected to the Legislature. In the deliberations of that body he took a most prominent part. His principal efforts were chronicled in the question of the railroad system of those days.   .

In 1852, he was elected to Congress, and in 1854, he was re-elected. During his first year he achieved a magnificent record; due principally to his telling speech against the Nebraska Bill. Senator Douglas paid him an eloquent compliment upon this occasion. He also assisted materially in that movement which gave about $2,000,000 worth of swamp lands to the State ; and favored the appropriation of $5,000,-000 for the deepening of the Illinois and Michigan Canal, a measure which was lost in the Senate.

In 1857, he was elected Judge of the Circuit Court, and served up to the summer of 1861. He subsequently declined re-election.

In 1862, he was re-elected to Congress.

In 1866, Mr. Norton came to Chicago. In this year, he was appointed U. S. Attorney, and held the office up to the spring of 1869. While United States Attorney, the records showed more convictions and a greater amount of monies collected than in any other State, except New York.

SAMUEL S. HAYES.

Samuel Snowden Hayes, the Comptroller of the City of Chicago, was born Dec. 25, 1820, in Nashville, Tennessee, where his father, Dr. R. P. Hayes, settled soon after his retirement from the Surgeonship of a New York regiment, engaged in the last conflict between the United States and Great Britain. Having acquired all the educational advantages a solicitous father could procure for his son, Mr. Hayes began active life as a store boy in a drug store ; was soon made a prescription clerk, and rose so rapidly subsequently, as, in a brief interval, to decline the entire charge of, and a partnership in, a drug store in Indiana. In August, 1838, he went into the drug business on his own account in Shawneetown, Illinois. The occupation proving incongenial, however, he abandoned it soon after for the legal profession. In the practice of law — he was admitted to the bar in 1842 — Mr. Hayes remained up to 1852, when, having caused the wilds of Mount Vernon and Carmi, Illinois, to ring with the music of his forensic efforts, he removed to Chicago. This was a sensible project.

Very early in life Mr. Hayes gave good promise of success in the political arena. The first demonstration, perhaps, was in 1843, when he took the stump in favor of the Democratic Party. In 1845, at the Memphis Convention, called for the promotion of Western and Southern interests, his speech for the coalition of parties elicited a high compliment from John C. Calhoun, whose expressions he con-

9

demned; in 1846 he was sent to the Legislature; in 1847 he was selected a delegate to a Convention for the Revision of the Constitution; and in 1848 he was constantly on the stump in Southern Illinois.

On his removal to Chicago, Mr. Hayes was employed by the City as Counsellor and City Solicitor. Senator Douglas, however, soon brought him from his seclusion, by proposing the repeal of the Missouri Compromise. This measure he opposed vehemently. His action brought forward Senator Douglas in 1855, when that statesman paid particular attention to Mr. Hayes and others. This fact to the contrary, notwithstanding, in obedience to the Democratic principle, no better supporter of Douglas, it is said, was afterwards found than Mr. Hayes. From this period up to and during the war of the Rebellion, the voice of our present Comptroller was always heard plainly in open convention.

The position assumed by Mr. Hayes when appointed Comptroller of Chicago, in 1862, was in the interest of economy and regularity so emphatically that the Council, on his withdrawal in 1865, gave him an unanimous vote of commendation. Shortly after, he was appointed one of the three members of the United States Revenue Commission. Messrs. Wells and Colwell were taken from the Republican Party, and Mr. Hayes from the Democratic. The financial report of Mr. Hayes, in this connection, elicited an editorial from the *London Times*. His reply ended as follows: "As far as the liabilities of the United States are concerned, they seem to me quite within our means of payment, without impoverishing our people, and without wronging our creditors."

AUTOBIOGRAPHY OF EGBERT JAMIESON.*

"Crede quod habes, et habes."

It may not be unnecessary to inform the reader that the following autobiography had its origin in a conversation between the author and the publisher, who did him the honor of calling several times upon him.

It appeared to me a favorable opportunity to undertake the task, and enriching myself with all the necessary material. I accordingly took advantage of it. I regret, however, that the very general curiosity of the public, with regard to the particulars of my history, could not have been satisfied at an earlier date — say on yesterday,— but its importance required rather a more detailed consideration than at that time I had any leisure to bestow upon it. Besides, the original memoirs in Spanish, prepared soon after my return from Europe, early last spring, were destroyed in the great fire of October, 1871, and hence it has been with no little difficulty that a correct recital of facts and occurrences has been prepared.

To begin, then. I had two parents — one of each kind — both "poor, but honest," and I have good reason to believe, and do most solemnly assert, that I was not ushered into this life on the European Plan. Consequently, my cradle was not surrounded by those prejudices and ideas of

*Note.— The city attorney having repeatedly declined to be interviewed, wrote his autobiography, at the request of the author of this work. It would not be fair to leave the gentleman out. — THE AUTHOR.

superiority with which pride and flattery always seek to
intoxicate the minds of the privileged classes.

It is a most extraordinary circumstance that the earliest
ancestor our family has any record of, superintended, with
the assistance of the princes of the line of the Pharoahs,
the building of those wonderful structures, the Pyramids.
Having completed this job, he next turned his attention to
life insurance, but in this he met with little or no success,
(the family cheek having then not sufficiently developed
itself,) and we next hear of him as a sutler in the army of
Cambyses Second, King of Persia, in his raid against the
Egyptians. During this campaign he was shot by his commander, there being at that time a great surplus of warriors,
and the railroad facilities for transporting them greatly
obstructed. This painful incident took place some five
hundred years before Christ, and none of the descendants
have felt like doing much since.

Coming down a trifle later, say about the fifteenth century, our family tree blossoms profusely with celebrated
musicians, with an occasional literary bud. It is related of
Claudin Gaimeisen, (an Italian, in the direct line), that in
1475, while playing an engagement in a horse car in Jersey
City, he caused a very spirited air to be sung, accompanying
himself with the accordion, which so animated a gentleman
who was present, that he clapped his hands on the person of
my ancestor,— a struggle ensued — and my deceased relative
was buried from the hospital on the next day.

Claudin left surviving him a widow of the name of
Jinkins, and two adopted children. William Henry, the
elder of the children, is said to have been a delicate youth,
and excessively fond of books; but the supply in general
literature was somewhat limited at home, being confined to
" HOYLE'S GAMES," and the " Life of James Buchanan." He
was accordingly sent at an early age to a Female Seminary,

where he graduated with distinguished honors. He was the author of numerous poems and tales; his chief production being " BETSEY AND I ARE OUT," — a passionate story of Italian incident, which was marked by such grandeur of thought and eloquence of expression, that it attracted for it great attention in " going the rounds of the press." In athletic sports he was a great enthusiast, and is said to have had few superiors. But at last, " vaulting ambition o'er-leaped itself," and in a hotly contested game of " freeze out," he took a severe cold, and shortly after expired in great agony.

For the next four hundred years the family history is too barren of incident to write about. It wants variety — it wants activity — it wants interest. If you do n't believe it, some one more interested in the matter than I am had better undertake the search.

In conclusion, it is but proper that the reader should be informed that my principal object in thus far divulging the important historical events which are here communicated to my fellow citizens, was to supply in some measure, the immense chasm which the absence of these memoirs may leave in the annals of our country. In so doing, I have to acknowledge my obligations to Captain Hickey, and Detectives Ellis and Dixon, for many valuable suggestions, but for reasons which I do not choose here to divulge, I have not availed myself of them, notwithstanding their absence may, to some extent, render the plan of my work incomplete.

\

JOSEPH K. C. FORREST.

The City Clerk, Mr. Forrest, was born in the city of Cork, Ireland, November 26, 1820, and was baptized in St. Ann's Shandon Church — " Bells of Shandon." His father, who resided in the city of Cork and vicinity for fifty years, was for thirty years director of one of the largest mercantile firms there — Cummins Brothers & Co. He acquired here a business education, and aside from his occupation in this particular branch of industry, farmed over six hundred acres of land, and conducted a large planing mill and tanyard. He was, as well, a freeman and burgess of the city. Mr. Forrest's uncle, Phillip Ryder, was for thirty years Comptroller of Customs for the port of Cork. His first cousin, Mr. P. R. Tivy, is married to a sister of Sir Thomas Lyons, formerly Mayor and Member of Parliament for Cork. His oldest brother, John L. Forrest, married a daughter of James Lane, Esq., formerly Mayor of the city of Cork. The subject of this sketch was a schoolmate of the late John Francis Maguire, Mayor and Member of Parliament for Cork.

Mr. Forrest came to Chicago July, 1840, and was introduced into society by Hon. J. Young Scammon, who continues to be his friend. After a short time, Mr. Forrest became associate editor of the *Journal*, with Riebel L. Wilson, Esq. He then became editor of the *Gem of the Prairie*, a weekly paper which was merged into the *Tribune*. In fact, it was at the urgent solicitation of Mr. Forrest, who was one of its founders, that this journal was so christened. The prospectus, however, was written by Mr. Wheeler, under the old heading Mr. Forrest subsequently sold his interest. In 1846-7, he went as associate editor upon Hon. John Wentworth's paper, the old *Democrat*, accepting the very large salary, at that time, of $1,000. While acting as editor, Mr. Forrest was elected Clerk of the Recorder's Court, vanquishing Hon. Philip A. Hoyne by over nine hundred votes. Hon. Daniel O'Hara, at present City Treasurer, was his successor in the office.

Mr. Forrest has written a great deal on Finance for the Press. He is at present engaged in a philosophical work on " The Nature of Life and Government," in which he combats the Darwinian theory, and the competitive theory of enlightened self-interest as set forth by Mill, Lecky, and other modern writers. He contends that the "body of thought" which has governed the civilized world from the time of Bacon to the present, and on which our great legal principles are founded, is in process of consummation; also, that the era, and the reign of force, and the power of great governments to control the social as they have heretofore the political state, is gradually asserting itself. In fact, he contends that the age of intellect, the power of man's intellect to control man, as held by Buckle and others, is fast fading away. He assumes that, ere long, the materialistic races of the world, such as the Anglo-Saxons and the Germans especially, will put the Church and the Latin races which are its chief support under the feet of the practical, or the State; that, as it was when Christ came first, the Romans were the masters of the world, so, when He comes the second time, the Germans, who are the modern counterparts of the ancient Romans, will be the rulers of the modern world.

Police and Fire Commissioners.

MARK SHERIDAN.

The Presidency of the Board of Police and Fire Commissioners has come unto Mr. Sheridan through a combination of circumstances never equaled in political history.
During his term he has observed the vanishing coat tails of
no less than five presidents : Brown, Talcott, Reno, Mason,
and Cleveland.　Brown resigned immediately after the great
fire ; Talcott threw up the sponge in a fit of horrible desperation — and he wrote his own death warrant ; Reno was
removed by the Medill administration, for daring to maintain the dignity of his position — and The People subsequently restored him ; Mason failed to " make a spoon, but
spoiled a horn," to use his own words ; and Cleveland was
ousted by the great political revolution.　Throughout the
same period, Mr. Sheridan was fighting Mayor Medill, the
Press, the entire Law Department, and Superintendent of Police Washburn ; narrowly escaping, by the way, an untimely
end from an inkstand in the hands of the mild and slim Police Superintendent.　During this unpleasantness, indeed, it
was broadly hinted that the assassination of the Commissioner
was meditated by somebody.　The idea sprung from the fact
that at one of the sessions of the Board of Police the desk
of the Secretary, Dr. Ward, was changed so as to completely
imprison Mr. Sheridan, in the event of open war.　Mr, Sheridan also saw the removal of Police Superintendents Kennedy and Washburn, Deputy Superintendent Sherman, Cap-
tains French, Fox and Lull ; the resignation and reinstate-

ment of Captain Hickey; and the removal of Fire Marshals
Williams, Schank and Walters. What he did *not* see of the
events that foreran and justified the remarkable political
revolution, would occupy a very small space indeed in this
batch of memoirs.

Police Commissioner Mark Sheridan was born in the
city of Waterford, Ireland, in 1826. At the age of fifteen, his father prosecuting a flourishing brewing traffic,
Mark entered the establishment as clerk and disburser.
This was his first idea of the business world; and the circumstances under which that idea was acquired were quite
arduous, the illness of his father placing the entire management of his extensive affairs on Mark's shoulders. He was
so engaged up to the revolutionary epoch in Irish history,
which numbered among its prominent spirits the names of
Smith, O'Brien, John Mitchell, and Thomas Francis Mea-
gher. At the first breath, Mr. Sheridan threw his whole
soul into the movement, and might have easily had a hempen
necklace if he did not escape to America under the protection of the flag of Norway. This prominent event in his life
occurred in 1848.

In this year he arrived in New York. Thence he proceeded to Philadelphia; thence to Baltimore. In those
localities, Mr. Sheridan, after repeated efforts, failed in finding reliable employment. He accordingly went to Missouri.
Here he built bridges. In Cincinnati he was more fortunate,
obtaining a railroad clerkship. In 1856 he came to Chicago,
and was identified, up to 1861, with packing interests. This
comprises the business record of the Commissioner.

Mr. Sheridan's political life has been a continuous series
of successes, this being his 'sixth election. He was first
elected overseer of highways. Re-elected, he declined the
unprofitable 'honor. Shortly afterward he was elected to
represent the fifth ward in the Common Council. His posi-

tion was very clearly defined as an alderman, on all subjects. Perhaps his attitude on the matter of assessment is one of his most noteworthy recollections. He held that the assess-ment of those days was decidedly inequitable, and clearly demonstrated it. He was re-elected Alderman for the third time, and had served about eighteen months of his last term, when elected Police Commissioner. On the organization of the new Board, under the new administration, he was elected its President. As President of the Board, Mr. Sheridan commands the strongest confidence of his colleagues, and of the great public.

E. F. C. KLOKKE

The history of this gentleman is a part and parcel of the antecedents of that great movement which swept chronic office holders completely out of existence. He was cheated badly out of his honors; only for a short time, however.

Police Commissioner E. F. C. Klokke was born in Holland in 1834. Up to the age of sixteen, his time was devoted to the securing of a mercantile education. In 1850, he came to New York, where he served his time at the hat trade.

In 1857, Mr. Klokke came to Chicago. He found it uphill work at this time, being the occasion, as old residents will remember, of a financial crisis. From the year of his arrival up to 1861, he filled position of bookkeeper and salesman alternately.

In this year Mr. Klokke entered the military service. At the first tap of the drum he had his name enrolled in the Ellsworth Zouaves, and when the call for 300,000 troops was made, he was one of the very first to march to the front, to the tune, "We are coming, Father Abraham." At this juncture he entered the Twenty-Fourth Illinois, joining the famous organization known as the Hecker Jaegers. He entered the service as a Lieutenant. Thence he was detached to the Signal Corps, and, as signal officer, served under Gen. Thomas, until 1864. His conduct for gallantry while thus engaged caused his promotion to a majorship.

On his return from the field, Mr. Klokke immediately resumed business and devoted his entire attention thereto up to July, 1871, when, upon the earnest solicitation of Mayor Medill, he accepted the position of Police Commissioner. At the fall election of same year he was elected by a majority of about 15,000.

In January, 1873, the difficulty arising between the Board of Police and the Superintendent of Police, touching the demoralizing twelve o'clock order — disapproved by the unanimous action of the Board — caused the removal of Mr. Klokke, and also Mr. Reno, from office, at the hands of Mayor Medill. Comment on Mr. Medill's action is rendered unnecessary by the fact that both of these gentlemen are returned to their old positions by the people. .

The prominence of Mr. Klokke in the grand programme which culminated in the overwhelming triumph of the People's movement gained his nomination to the position of Police Commissioner, at the hands of Mayor Colvin.

C. A. RENO.

Police Commissioner Reno was elected on the People's ticket to the position he now holds. He has paid but very little attention to politics. In 1859, however, he represented the Sixth Ward in the Common Council. He was born in Pennsylvania in 1818, November 17th. Up to 1845, in company with his father, Mr. Reno prosecuted a flourishing iron trade. Removing to Chicago in this year, he was the first man to devote himself exclusively to the sale of Briar Hill and Erie coal. The sales averaged, in these days, probably one hundred tons per day. As early as 1715, the Renos came over from France, to mine a lead-bank in St. Louis, and secured an extensive land grant. About 4,000 acres are yet left in Randolph County.

Mayor Medill nominated Mr. Reno, and the Council confirmed him. When the Board of Police, however, thought fit to suspend Mr. Washburn for conduct unbecoming an officer, Mayor Medill removed Mr. Reno in company with Mr. Klokke. What the people thought of it was shown at the election. Both Mr. Reno and Mr. Klokke are still Police Commissioners.

JAMES AYARS, Jr.

Mr. Ayars, having been almost unanimously nominated by the Board of Underwriters, was appointed Fire Commissioner by the Council, Nov. 10, 1873. The Commissioner was born in New Jersey in 1836, and at the age of 16 proceeded to New York. Here he was engaged for four years in the wholesale grocery trade. About this time he received an appointment to West Point. He did not accept it, however, but went to Covington, Kentucky, where his parents resided. Here, in 1858, he was admitted to the Bar, by Judge Moore, at present sitting in the Superior Court of Cook county. In 1862, he was elected County Clerk of Kenton county, Kentucky, and while serving was elected City Treasurer of Covington, for two terms, by a very large vote. In 1867, he came to Chicago, and entered the grain and insurance business, representing the "Phœnix" Insurance Company of Hartford, as local agent. On July 1, 1869, he was appointed Special Deputy of Customs. On Dec. 1, 1872, he resigned and returned to his insurance agency. He is not a People's ticket man. In deference to friendship for Mr. Philip Wadsworth, he accepted a position on the Executive Committee of the Citizen's Union ticket.

During the war, the Commissioner was a Captain of a battery attached to the 41st Kentucky Volunteers, and witnessed considerable guerilla warfare.

10

DR. WARD.

The Secretary of the Board of Police and Fire Commissioners, Dr. Ward, — this is the name by which he is best known,— was born at Pittsfield, Mass., December 9, 1823, and graduated in medicine at the Berkshire Medical college in 1845. In 1847, he removed to Chicago, and in January, 1855, he permanently settled here. He was a deputy in the office of the Clerk of the County Court of Cook county, for nine years — eight years in charge of the Probate department ; was principal clerk in the County Treasurer's office for two years, and has been Secretary of the Board for seven years. His usefulness here is a matter well recognized by all with whom he has been brought in contact.

Police Superintendent and Captains.

JACOB REHM.

The Superintendent of the pretty thoroughly reconstructed police force of the city of Chicago is Jacob Rehm; this being the third time he has been called upon to assume so responsible a position.

Mr. Rehm was born near Strasbourg, in the province of Alsace, in 1828, and is of German descent. The place of his birth is a French possession, yet its inhabitants speak the German tongue. In his native place, Mr. Rehm remained at school up to the age of 12. In 1840, the family removed to Chicago. Here the subject of this sketch has lived ever since, excepting a brief stay in Dupage county.

In early life, Mr. Rehm pursued a miscellaneous career; as in fact did a great many people who entered Chicago at so undeveloped a period. His first experience in police life occurred in 1851. In this year he joined the force as a patrolman — in the days of James L.'Howe, who was City Marshal. As patrolman, Mr. Rehm served on the force up to 1855, when he accepted a Street Commissionership in the North Division. One year's service — the term for which he was elected — was succeeded by an appointment as Foreman of Street Improvement under the Superintendent of Public Works. His experience here, with the recollection of his police service, may be said to have thoroughly initiated him into public life, as upon his retirement he was appointed City Marshal, or Chief of Police. Two years after, however, he left the force and entered the service of Lill & Diversy, brewers. In the spring of 1861, on the organization of the police force after the Metropolitan system, police life assumed a resistless attraction, and Mr. Rehm accepted the Deputy Superintendency under the new law.

Resigning, he once more entered the service of Lill & Diversy. The old love was strong, nevertheless. Accordingly Mr. Rehm went back to the force again, assuming the position of Superintendent. While acting as such, in 1863, he was elected County Treasurer. In 1866, he, once more, was appointed Superintendent of Police. The office he filled up to 1869, in which year he resigned, to be succeeded by ex-Superintendent Kennedy. This comprised Superintendent Rehm's police experience up to his present appointment. The experiences of a Chief of Police during his successive terms of office would form volumes of criminal history. The sudden growth of a great city invariably multiplies the agents of crime, and no city observed a better illustration of the fact.

After the appointment of Mr. Kennedy, Mr. Rehm accepted a position in the United States Revenue office in this city. He then entered the malt business on his own account, which has proven very successful. His establishment still stands in the vicinity of Clybourne Avenue Bridge.

WILLIAM BUCKLEY.

The Captain of the First District of Police was born in Ballyhone, parish of Afhane, county of Waterford, Ireland, June 9, 1832, and is therefore about 41 years of age. In 1848 — at the age of 16 — having spent his early life at school, he emigrated and came to New York, where he went to work on the farm of Col. George D. Coles, of Glencoe, Queen's county, at a salary of $10 per month. In 1856, having spent a short time on a farm in Warren county, Ohio, the Captain came to Chicago. He now was placed in charge of the coal business of Col. R. J. Hamilton, and subsequently engaged in the same business for Law & Strother. A little experience as a car-driver and conductor followed. He then joined the police force in 1865. Promotion rapidly followed. As Roundsman, Station-Keeper, and Sergeant, Mr. Buckley's conduct won for him early, on the resignation of Capt. Hickey, the position of Captain, which he obtained July 14, 1873, receiving the unanimous confirmation of the Council. Among other experiences, Capt. Buckley narrowly escaped assassination at the hands of the supposed murderers of McKeaver, killed in the race between "Butler" and "Cooley," on the turf; was dragged under a private carriage by a contumacious driver at the time of the Sanitary Fair in Chicago; and received a severe pummeling at the hands of roughs while returning from St. John's Church with his wife, March 10, 1871. He tells with gusto a great many experiences with soldiers, returning from the war of the rebellion.

M. C. HICKEY.

Capt. Michael C. Hickey, of the Second District, was born near the city of Limerick, Ireland, April 18, 1826. The close proximity of the Captain's birthplace to that city, so deservedly famed for the beauty of her daughters, afforded him excellent opportunities to revel repeatedly in love's young and festive dream. His susceptibilities were not inclined that way, however. The path that lay before him he perceived was one he should construct with his own head and his own hands. At the age of 18 he accordingly bid adieu to the environs of fair Limerick, and crossed the broad ocean to toil.

Arriving in Boston, Massachusetts, the Captain apprenticed himself to the plumbing and gas-fitting trades. Four years of a stay here satisfied him that he might do better. He therefore, in 1848, came to Chicago. Up to 1853 he directed his energies to meat interests, acquiring all convenient acquaintances in the meantime. In this year he was elected Constable of the Fourth Ward; performing, at the same time, police duty. In 1855 he was elected County Constable. Immediately afterward he was elected Justice of the Peace, and acted as such up to 1858. It now came to pass that in an effort to be re-elected, he was defeated. From 1858 up to 1861, he consequently built sewers under the firm name of Farrell & Hickey, and did extraordinarily well for that period.

In 1861 he joined the police force as a patrolman. Two

'months had hardly elapsed before he was created a Sergeant. The position in those days was not an enviable one, the incumbent being required to take care of his men during all the hours of the night, and at an era in Chicago's history when crime stalked terrorless in broad daylight. The beat allotted to Capt. Hickey out-deviled any in Chicago, embracing the region of which such filthy purlieus as Griswold street formed the unattractive center. In this vicinity in 1862 he was shot by burglars, and it was only after five months of the best surgical treatment that his life was saved. He had just recovered when he narrowly escaped being crushed to death between two cars on State street.

On January 1, 1866, he was appointed Captain. As such it is said he has been instrumental in sending about 500 evil-doers to the Penitentiary — among them the six masked ruffians interested in the Jefferson-Snell robbery; and Corbett, Flemming, and Kennedy, the perpetrators of the Cicero murder, to the gallows.

I

FREDERICK GUND.

Capt. Gund was born in Planckstadt, Baden, Germany, December 1, 1823. At the age of 17 he was sent to a military school at Mannheim, according to the commendable custom in vogue in Germany. After six years, impressed with the attractiveness of a republican form of government, he came to America and engaged in tobacco manufacture. In 1847 he came to Chicago. In 1854 he joined the police force, and was appointed a Lieutenant under Dyer. In 1863 he was appointed Captain of the North Side. In 1865 he was elected a Police Commissioner. At the expiration of his term he was appointed Captain.

The duties devolving upon Capt. Gund lie among the Germans mainly; and the best endorsement is their entire confidence in the Captain.

FIRE MARSHALS.

MATTHIAS BENNER.

The Chief Fire Marshal is Matthias Benner. He was born in Lauffeldt, Germany, and came to America in 1848, settling within nine miles of Port Washington, Wisconsin. In May 5, 1851, he came to Chicago, his family taking up an economical abode on State street, near Harrison. The chief, upon his arrival, entered a cigar shop, and subsequently engaged in the trunk business, where he remained for nine months. In the meantime, there were very few large fires by night he did not attend, ringing No. 7's bell when anything "showed up." In these expeditions he served on Hook and Ladder No. 1.

He was not a regular member of the fire department until arrived at the age of eighteen. He was duly elected about October 10, 1856. He remained a member up to April 5, 1859. He then joined the Enterprise No. 2. He then went for six months to St. Louis. In March, 1860, however, throughthe misrepresentation of a politician, it is stated, Mr. Benner was removed from the force. Subsequently, he was invited back by Chief U. P. Harris, but declined. He eventually accepted a position on Hook and Ladder No. 1. In a short time, he was transferred to the foremanship of the Island Queen, which he held up to April 1, 1861. Afterwards, Mr. Benner, at the request of Mr. Harris, took charge of the Long John. But at his own request, he was made a private, to attend a night school. The school shortly failing, he, at the request of the Board of Police, was assigned to the charge of Enterprise No. 2. This position he held until May 4, 1868. He was now appointed by the Commissioners Third Assistant. He filled the position up to March, 1871. Then he was appointed First Assistant, which he filled up to the time he was appointed Chief, *vice* Williams, removed.

The record of the Chief is truly an eventful one; and it is certain nobody was more surprised than himself when he was appointed Chief Fire Marshal.

Mr. Benner, in November and December, made an extensive inspection tour for the purpose of improving his department. Among other places, he visited Pittsburgh, Washington, Baltimore, Philadelphia, New York, Brooklyn and Boston; also, the Amoskeag Works, and the Seneca Falls establishment. The result of his visits will probably be a great improvement in the Fire Department; satisfactory to himself, and advantageous to the public.

DENIS J. SWENIE.

The First Assistant Fire Marshal was born in the city of Glasgow, Scotland, in the year 1834, where he remained until he arrived at the age of fourteen. In 1848 he came to Chicago and engaged in the harness trade. This engrossed his attention up to the year of 1859. In the meantime Mr. Swenie was a member of the volunteer fire department, running "wid der masheen" more for sport than anything else. In 1849 he entered the service as a hose boy on No. 3, stationed at that time on the corner of Wells and Kinzie streets. He subsequently joined the regular engine corps. In 1852 Mr. Swenie went on the "Red Jacket," and took the position of Assistant Foreman. In 1854 the company was disbanded. Mr. Swenie then returned to No. 3. It was now that his services became appreciated. In 1856 he was appointed First Assistent Engineer. In 1858 he was appointed Chief Engineer, organizing the paid steam fire department.

In those days the position of Mr. Swenie was anything but enviable. The volunteer department considered the organization of a paid department as a slur upon their honor, and fought with a desperation worthy of a better cause. All those squabbles, memorable in the annals of our fire history, Mr. Sweenie successfully mastered.

In 1861 Mr. Swenie took command of the Liberty, stationed on North Dearborn street. In 1867 the same company accompanied him to the command of the Gund. He

was captain of this company when appointed First Assistant
Fire Marshal, October 1, 1873.

In all the great fires of his days the First Assistant Fire
Marshal participated; among others, the great fire of 1857.
On this occasion, Mr. Swenie took charge of the diggers,
and recovered eighteen bodies out of twenty-three supposed
to have been lost. His traveling in pursuit of interesting
information to further the interests of the Fire Department is extensive; and there are a great many who rank
Mr. Swenie to-day among the foremost firemen of the
country, from the extent of his experience.

In the great fire, Marshal Swenie, taking charge of affairs
on the North Side, saved, it is said, five entire blocks in the
vicinity of Kinzie street bridge. The engines in action at
the time were Nos. 11, 5, and 16.

CHARLES S. PETRIE.

The Second Assistant is Charles S. Petrie. He was born in Chicago, Sept. 25, 1840, and studied at the Kinzie Public School. His educational course was further extended by a term at St. Joseph's Catholic School in this city, and afterwards at South Bend. At the age of 13, or thereabouts, he went to work at Fuller's old light - house. Here he was employed for about three years. He then went into McCormick's manufacturing establishment, and then into Wright's machine shop. In the meantime, he served in the Volunteer Fire Department. He now went South, and served as Assistant Engineer on the Mississippi. At the breaking out of the war he returned to Chicago, and joined the Steam Fire Department, serving as stoker on Engine 3. In 1866, he went upon the " Rice " as stoker. Thence he was promoted to the engineership. He was then appointed Engineer on No. 3, the " James."

In 1872, he was promoted to the position of Third Assistant, and in the same year to .the Second Assistantship. It is in the mechanical department Mr. Petrie's energies are most felt.

11

/

WILLIAM MUSHAM.

This gentleman is Third Assistant Fire Marshal. He was born in the city of Chicago, Feb. 9, 1839. In February, 1855, he joined the Volunteer Fire Department — at the early age of 16. Meantime, he pursued his avocation as a carpenter. About 1861, Mr. Musham joined the Paid Fire Department, which, at that time, was about fully organized. The first engine our subject went upon was the " Little Giant," located on the corner of Washington and Dearborn streets. He served here as a pipeman. He was then transferred to the " Atlantic," corner of State and Michigan streets. Having served here for a time, he was transferred to the " Giant," but after a short time, resigned and went to Philadelphia, where he served on the Volunteer Department, on the engine " Fairmount." Returning to Chicago, he went upon the " T. B. Brown," on West Lake street. Here he served as assistant foreman up to 1868. He now went as Foreman upon the " Giant," located at this time upon Maxwell street. After the great fire, March 1, 1872, Mr. Musham was appointed Third Assistant Fire Marshal.

The experience of Mr. Musham on our Fire Department is quite varied; among other adventures, suffering severe injuries by the falling of a wall at a fire, corner of LaSalle and Water streets, in 1865, where two firemen were killed.

MAURICE W. SHAY.

The Fourth Assistant Fire Marshal is Maurice W. Shay. He was born in Nova Scotia, in 1832, and, as early as 1838, came to Eastport, Maine, remembering the great fire in that city in 1839, which destroyed three-quarters of a mile of property, including many wharves and much shipping. In 1840 he went to Charlestown, Massachusetts. In that city, in 1847, he ran with the "Warren" engine company, and with that company went to Boston and participated in the Haverill street fire, which destroyed three squares. In 1849 he went to Cleveland, Ohio, and in 1850 joined "Phœnix" engine company. In 1852, he was a member of the Eagle Fire Department in Pittsburgh. In 1855 he was elected Assistant Foreman of the company. In 1856 he was elected Assistant Engineer of the Cleveland Fire Department, He participated in the New England fire in that city.

Mr. Shay then came to Chicago. Here his old love accompanied him. In 1857 he joined the Liberty Hose Company, No. 6, as a pipeman. In 1858 he was appointed Assistant Foreman. In 1861 he joined the Paid Fire Department as a truckman on Hook and Ladder No. 1. In 1862 he was transferred to engine 6, the "Little Giant." In 1864 he was appointed Foreman of engine company No. 9, the "Sherman." In 1867 he accepted the foremanship of No. 13, the "Titsworth." Here he stayed until detailed Assistant Fire Marshal, in October, 1873. In all the great fires of his days Mr. Shay participated, with high honors.

LEO MEYERS.

The Fifth Assistant Marshal is Leo Meyers, aged about thirty-nine, of French extraction; was born on the North Side, and is distinguished by the reputation of being the Chesterfield of the Fire Department. He is very popular. Mr. Meyers joined the Volunteer Fire Department probably at the age of fourteen, and, up to the organization of the Fire Department, followed iron moulding, being for some time foreman in Letz' foundry. He first served as a torch boy on No. 3, the "Niagara;" became Foreman of the "Island Queen;" held the same position on the "U. P. Harris;" was at one time Assistant Engineer under U. P. Harris; and also served as Foreman of the "Tempest Hose" and of the "Babcock." On October 5, 1873, he was appointed Marshal under Chief Benner.

J. J. WADE,

95 South Desplaines street, a prominent plumber and gas fitter, has gotten up a Hydrogen Gas Machine, which is beneficial to the public in the fitting up of buildings where tanks are in use, as there is no fire connected with it, and the lead is put together without the use of solder, therefore saving from thirty to forty per cent. in labor and material. This machine is indispensable in the fitting up of chemical, vinegar, distilling, and other works where acids are in use.

The value of the instrument is enhanced by the fact that it lessens the liability to fire in large public buildings. Mr. Wade has been connected with the plumbing and gas fitting interests of Chicago for over sixteen years, and has accomplished the work on our most prominent public structures.

Board of Public Works.

REDMOND PRINDIVILLE.

Mr. Prindiville was born in the southern part of Ireland, in 1826, of parents of the purest description of Norman about them. His father and uncle took degrees in Trinity. At a very early age, Redmond was borne to the State of New York, whence he was removed to Michigan for a time, to suit the convenience of the family, most probably. At nine, he entered Chicago. From this time up to 1849, it might be said that Redmond divided his days between sailing and attending school; holding a captaincy at 17, and until he was 23. He now connected himself with the Galena Railroad; and in various positions he remained in the service of this corporation up to 1855, when he resigned. Since, Mr. Prindiville has identified himself extensively with river interests, owning, at the present, considerable shipping. He was appointed to the Board in December, 1869. He served in the Council from 1860 to '62, from the then Eighth Ward.

WILLIAM H. CARTER.

Commissioner Carter was born in Lancaster, Worcester county, Massachusetts, in 1821. He is, accordingly, 53 years of age. When about eight years old, Mr. Carter went to Franklin county, and worked there diligently on a farm for some time. He went to school there, and subsequently to the Academy at East Hampton, Massachusetts. He thence went to Springfield, in the same State, and engaged in building. He was at this time but 20. He went now to Northampton, and built there, among other structures, the House of Correction.

In the Fall of 1853, Mr. Carter came to Chicago, and pursued building up to the time of his election to the Council, where he served in 1855 and 1856. In 1857, he served on the Board of Education. In February, 1868, he was elected a member of the Board of Public Works.

He retired with the success of the People's Party; giving place to Louis Wahl.

J. K. THOMPSON.

Mr. Thompson was born in Cincinnati, Ohio, in 1816, and followed building up to 1857. In July, 1855, he came to Chicago. In March, 1857, Mr. Thompson, was given the full control of bridges and public buildings. In 1861, when the Board was organized, he was appointed Superintendent of Streets and Public Buildings, a position he has filled with great ability. He is the parent of the present style of bridges.

In his peculiar sphere Commissioner Thompson, it is said, stands without an equal. It has been intimated that a desideratum, municipally, would be an Inspector of Public Buildings. If such an office were made, it would, most probably, be tendered to Mr. Thompson.

LOUIS WAHL.

Louis Wahl, over whose selection as a member of the Board of Public Works so much of a stir was made in the Common Council, was born at Pirmassens, in Rhenish Bavaria, in 1830. He is of pure German extraction, and his connections, wherever found, rank very high in society. His father was attached to the Bavarian Crown in the capacity of tax collector, and his uncles at one time represented five million francs in Paris, France. One of those relatives is at present Superintendent of the Road from Paris to the Mediterranean. He was probably the only prominent German who, during the unpleasantness between France and Prussia, was not hustled out of Paris.

In 1847, the Wahl family, removing to America, Mr. Louis Wahl's father entered the glue business in Milwaukee, and achieved an independent fortune. The business, like many other foreigners upon their arrival on these shores, he picked up accidentally, and established. His success may be judged from the fact that he left, as an inheritance to his sons, the magnificent sum of $200,000. Besides this, he established the facilities for a glue house in Chicago for them. In 1850 Louis Wahl, in company with his brother Christian, took a portion of the fortune left them and made the trip to California; and it might be said passed through the Golden Gate to amass a fortune in Chicago.

They came to this city in 1854. The first place they constructed their glue works (their father's success having urged them to *stick* to glue) was on the North Branch. In 1856 they removed to their present location, situated on Broad street near Thirty-first. At the outset they sent out 50,000 pounds of glue annually. Their present production is 3,000,000 pounds; the amount of capital invested is $600,-000, and their business is probably the largest in the world.

The political position of Louis Wahl has been on the Republican side; though he cast his first vote for Pierce in 1852. He never cared much for office, on account of the immense requirements of his business. Among the positions of trust he held, however, was a position in the State Legislature, and a Commissionership of Bridewell. A great effort was also made to run him for Mayor in last fall's election, on the Citizen's Union ticket.

His election to the Board of Public Works was bitterly opposed, on account of his presumed connection with an effort to once bribe the Aldermen in reference to the Ford contract. It is stated, nevertheless, that Mr. Wahl knew nothing of the attempt; handing over to a certain party a certain sum of money, with no knowledge whatever of its disposition. This money reached certain Aldermen, it appears, subsequently. The probable presumption of Mr. Wahl was that it was merely a present to an editor for the influence of his newspaper.

BOARD OF HEALTH.

DR. HAHN.

Dr. Hahn, the President of the Board of Health, was born in the east. He graduated in Jefferson Medical College, and for a time was connected, as a resident physician, in Blockley College, of Philadelphia. He subsequently removed to Chicago.

The Doctor's experience, as spoken of in Chicago, is ranked among that of the highest in the profession.

Among other political positions he has held that of an alderman.

12

CHARLES E. MOORE.

Charles E. Moore was born in Dublin, Ireland, in 1825. In 1837 he went to Albany, N. Y., where he remained until 1848. Here he learned the trade of masonry. While here he was a member of the Emmett Guards, and offered his services in the Mexican war, with that organization. They were not called out, however.

In 1848, Mr. Moore came to Chicago and worked at his trade. In 1860 he made the trip to Pike's Peak. Returning in 1861, he entered the army, and for three years and three months served as Major of the 23d, which, in company with Col. Mulligan and others, he helped in organizing.

Among the positions of public trust he has filled were the Aldermanship of the Seventh Ward and Police Judgeship. Resigning the latter, he was subsequently chosen to the Board of Health.

GEORGE SCHLŒTZER.

This gentleman was born in Kusel, Rhenish Bavaria, and is 52 years of age. His early life was spent in a very classical atmosphere; which the observer of the Doctor's habits and predilections to-day may easily surmise. His father was the chief medical officer in the Bavarian army, at one time, and participated therewith in the Russian campaign.

Educated in Munich, Dr. Schlœtzer practiced medicine in the locality of that name as well as in Prague and Brussels, and very considerably throughout all Germany. He came to Chicago fifteen years ago, and has devoted himself to his practice ever since. He entered the Board of Health in 1869; was the City Physician at one time; and is at present connected with the Protestant Diaconese Hospital.

BEN. C. MILLER.

Dr. Miller was born in Putnam county, Indiana, and having received an academical education at Battle Ground, Indiana, joined the army at 17 — Company K, 10th Indiana Cavalry; rising from the ranks to a First Lieutenantcy, in the Army of the Cumberland. In 1865 Ben. studied medicine in his father's office, and soon graduated at Rush Medical College. He then entered Cook County Hospital, and in 1869 was appointed County Physician.

Dr. Miller was appointed Superintendent of Public Charities for Cook county in 1872. In this position he effected incalculable good, especially in the matter of hospitals. A comparison of the expenditures of his year and of the year previous shows a reduction in his favor of over $100,000. He was subsequently selected to his present office — the Health Superintendency. Here he has perfected the present admirable vaccination regulations.

JOSEPH McDERMOTT.

Joseph McDermott was born in Durrow, King's county, Ireland, in 1827. When arrived at the age of twenty, he came to this country, and settled in New York, in the liquor traffic. After a successful experience there, he came to Chicago, and resumed the same business. He is engaged therein at present.

Politically, Mr. McDermott is a Democrat. He never sought office much, and his selection to the Board of Health probably surprised him somewhat.

MR. MOSES HOOK.— This gentleman has also just been elected to the Board of Health.

POLICE JUSTICES AND CLERK.

DANIEL SCULLY.

The name of Daniel Scully is a household word in a very large region. There never was a more efficient Justice elected in the city of Chicago.

Mr. Scully was born in the city of New York, March 28, 1839. When the boy was two years old, his parents removed to McHenry county. Here the old folks placed him in charge of the farm. Agricultural pursuits were not sympathetic with the disposition of the Judge. He looked for better things.

In those days it was habitual with men of remarkable proclivities to get all the information they could. With this end in view, the Judge, in the year 1860, devoted himself to teaching school. The more he taught, the more he became convinced that he needed to learn something himself. His education he considered simply fortuitous. So it was. Accordingly, in the fall of 1860, Mr. Scully went to St. Mary's of the Lake. Here he graduated, after two years, in the scientific and commercial departments. His conduct here elicited a very complimentary notice from Dr. McMullen, the principal of the institution.

In 1863 and 1864 Judge Scully studied law in the Chicago Law School, under the control of Judge Booth, at present of the Circuit Court. When graduated, he received a handsome compliment from the principal, being the only one out of a class of thirty-four who had not been in a law office.

A promiscuous line of life followed his honors. The educational seemed to have the mastery, however. Having graduated in law, Mr. Scully made a tour of Iowa and Minnesota; but failing to discover any favorable locality wherein to throw out his shingle, he came to Chicago. He now entered the office of Willard & Quinn, and devoted himself rigidly to study. The result was a success that promises to be permanent.

The Judge has been appointed Police Justice three times by an overwhelming vote. Among other honors, he has served Hartland, in McHenry county, as Town Supervisor.

H. A. KAUFMANN.

The Justice of the North Division Police Court is Henry Aaron Kaufmann, a gentleman whose admirers north of the river, it is said, are very numerous. His progress so far in public life, it is certain, is only the result of an industrious attention to the minutest details of the various stations in life allotted to him.

Mr. Kaufmann was born in Hesse-Darmstadt, in 1821. Early in life, conceiving an idea that a young and rising region possessed availabilities not discoverable elsewhere, Mr. Kaufmann came to America, and, after prospecting somewhat, settled in Chicago.

His first introduction to public life, it may be said, was while employed by the city as a police patrolman and detective. Thus engaged, Mr. Kaufmann enjoyed ample opportunities for forming friendships — acquisitions he succeeded admirably in securing.

Being moderately ambitious, Mr. Kaufmann, subsequent to his retirement from the police force, was elected a Town Supervisor. The next prominent office of public trust awaiting him was the Police Justiceship of the North Division.

MARTIN SCULLY.

The Clerk of the South Side Police Court is Martin Scully. He was born in the county of Tipperary, Ireland, in 1835. In 1851 he emigrated to America, and learned the moulding business. This avocation he pursued up to his election. When the war broke out Mr. Scully entered the 23d Illinois regiment, under Mulligan, and was very soon appointed Sergeant of Company K. When the siege of Lexington took place, Sergeant Scully succeeded in showing an extraordinary hand, turning out 1,600 weight of shot from a rebel foundry at the time of the bombardment. He was here captured, but was subsequently exchanged, among the Camp Jackson prisoners. In 1861 he was mustered out at St. Louis. Returning to Chicago, in company with Capt. Shanley he raised a company and took 100 men to the famous Sixty-Ninth, the Irish regiment. Promotion soon followed, serving at the battle of Fair Oaks as Second Lieutenant. After the battle of Antietam he was appointed Captain. At Fair Oaks Mr. Scully was wounded. He was present also at the seven days fight under Gen. McClellan. The history of Capt. Scully can be learned at a glance when it is told that himself and two others were the sole survivors of Company D, of the Sixty-Ninth. When the Fenian excitement broke out, Capt. Scully went to Ireland, and was arrested in the city of Cork. Returning in 1869, he was elected Clerk of the North Side Police Court. In 1873 he was elected Chief Clerk on the People's ticket. Aside from his political history, Mr. Scully has always taken an active part in the interests of the working men.

COLLECTORS AND ASSESSORS.

GEORGE VON HOLLEN.

This gentleman is the City Collector. He was born in the village of Drifthsethe, in Hanover, Germany, March 2, 1834, and, up to the age of fifteen, devoted himself to farming. At this age he left Fatherland, arriving in New York in 1849. Here he gave his services to a grocer, and subsequently to a butcher. In 1854, he came to Chicago. Here he resumed the business prosecuted in the east. Being a first-class Republican, Mr. Von Hollen soon became thoroughly identified with politics. From 1863 to 1865, he represented the Eleventh Ward in the Common Council. At the expiration of his term, he entered the Post-office and acted as foreman of foreign and general delivery. In 1869, he was a candidate for City Collector on the Republican ticket, but was defeated. In September, 1870, he was appointed a member of the Board of Health. This position he resigned in 1871, when elected on the Fire-proof ticket to the position of City Collector. His majority was over 6,000. In 1873, espousing the People's ticket, he was re-elected by a majority of over 10,000.

The experience of Mr. Von Hollen during the war, for his adopted country, was not very pleasant. Among other tribulations, he was captured by Morgan's guerillas while administering to the wounded and sick boys of the Twenty-Fourth Illinois, after the battle of Perryville, Kentucky. In this engagement, his brother, Bernhard, was killed.

In 1868, Mr. Von Hollen was elected President of the

North Side Turner Society, of which he is a distinguished member.

It is very rarely found that the dry duties of a City Collector correspond with the divine affinities of the poet. Mr. Von Hollen, nevertheless, has written some of the very finest kind of German and English verses, about one hundred of which have graced the colums of the *Staats Zeitung*.

COL. P. M. CLEARY.

The gentleman whose familiar name is observed at the top of this page is Collector for the South Town of Chicago. He was elected to his position April 1, 1873, by a majority of about 1,100.

He was born in Nanagh, county of Tipperary, Ireland, April 6, 1826, and arrived on these shores as long as 32 years ago. Five years of life in New York sufficed for an eager spirit like the Colonel's. The clattering wheel and the vulgar jostle were fresh variety when contrasted with the every-day life of his native town of Nanagh. But the combination grew monotonous, at length. Col. Cleary resolved to see the world. He accordingly selected Chicago as the starting-point. He had an uncle in this city, in the drug business; and this in itself was as great an inducement as a man of his push needed, to try his fortune in a strange city.

Here, fortune seemed to smile upon him at the outset. He found here a host of friends just like himself — genial, broad-hearted, and energetic. What go-aheadativeness he did not bring with him he procured with the least possible trouble. He entered real estate speculation when he had secured a good footing, and to this industry he still devotes the efforts of his matured business talent. Occasionally, the Colonel takes a trip to Europe, and, when he returns, dwells with ecstacy upon the many scenes he has observed there.

The Colonel's acquaintances tell stories of his adventures

13

during the war, that have beguiled the hours beside many a pleasant fireside. Those narratives it is not the province of the writer to rehearse, however.

Since his election to his present position, Col. Cleary has achieved a reputation as Collector that has elicited the unqualified approbation of the Press, having successfully moved upon the banks which manifested so sturdy a desire to resist payment.

LAURENCE O'BRIEN.

This gentlemen is the Collector of the West-Town of Chicago, and was elected April 1, 1873, on the Citizens' ticket, by a majority of 323.   By-the-way, it was rather a coincidence that the three town collectors elected that day were all Irishmen — Cleary, O'Brien, and Murphy.

Mr. O'Brien was born in the town of Newport, in Tipperary, Ireland, about the year 1836.   At the age of 17, our subject, with an eye to sport of the good old Irish style, left his native town and took a stroll through Leinster, Kildare, and other places of historic note in Ireland.   Among other spots visited, Mr. O'Brien paid his respects to the Curragh, the Heath of Marlborough, the Castle of Lord Nace, late Governor of India, and the beautiful strawberry beds of Dublin.

Mr. O'Brien served four years in the Irish constabulary, but was forced to leave on account of his nationalistic principles.   In Ireland, our subject followed baking, which trade he there acquired.   Since his advent to America, he has devoted himself mainly to the liquor traffic.

JOHN MURPHY.

This gentleman is Collector for the north town of Chicago, and was elected on the Workingman's ticket. He was born in the borough of Ross, County Wexford, Ireland, in 1841, and left at the age of fifteen years, coming directly to Chicago, where he worked, up to the fall of 1860, as a machinist. He then went to Pike's Peak, where he flourished; a great many, having been driven thither by the well remembered gold fever, returning disheartened. Mr. Murphy now returned to Chicago, intending to return to Pike's Peak with a set of machinery. The war of the Rebellion waxing warmly, however, at the time, he concluded to fight for his adopted country. Raising a company of three months troops, he was elected Second Lieutenant in the 67th Illinois, of which Mr. Hough was Colonel, and was detached to guard the prisoners at Camp Douglas. Thence he was detached to raise a company for the 90th Illinois. Raising Company G, he was elected its Captain, and in the following November proceeded to the field. Assigned to Gen. Denver's division, the Captain was ordered to LaGrange, Tennessee, to protect the Memphis and Charleston road. He went thence to Coldwater, Mississippi, where an engagement was had, wherein Gen. Van Dorn met his first repulse; to Lafayette, Tennessee; to Vicksburg, where he was present during the seige; to the battle of Mission Ridge, where his canteen was shot off him; to Knoxville, Tennessee, through a barren country, to meet Longstreet, who withdrew at the sight of the blue; to Chattanooga; and then to Atlanta with Sherman. Then came the battle of Dallas, where the company, with Company H, under command of Captain Murphy, were placed on the extreme right, with orders to fall back in case the Rebels charged. A charge was made, and the skirmish line to the left wavered. Yet the two companies under Murphy held the line in constant skirmish from nine o'clock in the evening until ten o'clock in the morning. The Rebels, supposing from the scattering fire kept up that all of the boys were there, fell back.

The Captain's company also participated when McPherson was killed, and lost in the engagement their knapsacks, cherished photographs, etc. Subsequently, when, the lines clashing, a hand-to-hand fight ensued, the 48th Illinois were knocked out of position, Murphy cried out to the 90th himself, and the result was a most desperate charge; plunging through the broken columns of the 48th, killing or capturing every man of the enemy, and appropriating six stands of colors. All through this campaign the gallantry of Captain Murphy was well recognized, and when mustered out in June, 1865, he was loaded down with honors.

CHARLES DENNEHY.

Charles Dennehy took a prominent part in the organization of the People's Party. His counsels and influence
went a good ways to form a rational and conservative
platform. Mr. Dennehy, it is understood, was one of
the number who called the first meeting and laid the
foundation for the new party. The difficulties to be encountered were, to harmonize conflicting elements and
reconcile men who, for years past, had been bitter political
opponents. It was apparent to him, as to others, that the
only sure road to success was to unite the liberal American,
Irish, and German people on one common platform, regardless of former political affiliations. .

Mr. Dennehy being known as a thorough representative Irishman, combined with his personal popularity
with all classes of citizens, the People's Party unanimously placed his name on their ticket for the important
position of City Assessor. As an evidence of the high esteem in which he is held by his fellow citizens, he ran very
strongly upon his ticket. It is needless to say that no better
selection could have been made for the discharge of the important duties of the office to which he has been elected.

Mr. Dennehy possessing the adventurous spirit of his race,
emigrated from County Kerry, Ireland, in the 17th year of
his age, to this country. He has lived in Chicago for the
past twenty years, and by his honesty, industry, and business
tact has acquired a liberal fortune. He is now a member of

the well-known firm of Weadly, Dennehy & Cleary, a reliable and leading wholesale liquor house.   During the past
four years, he has filled the office of North Town Assessor,
to the perfect satisfaction of all.   His knowledge of real
estate and his unblemished character pre-eminently qualify
him for the very responsible position to which he has been
so handsomely elected by the people.

EDWARD PHILLIPS.

Mr. Phillips, Assessor of the South Town of Chicago, was born in the County of Cavan, Ireland, in 1837. In 1840, he left his native place, and went to Schenectady, New York. After a stay of five years there, he went to the city of New York. The Phillips family had not been settled comfortably in the metropolis more than four years, it seems, when a westward yearning brought them inevitably to Chicago. The boy declined to come as yet, however. He desired a little more experience in life in the great city. Five years more of it induced him to pack up also, and come west.

No sooner had he arrived than his adventurous spirit enlisted him in the ranks of Fire Company No. 6, where he ran with Ex-Fire Marshal Williams, Capt. Connors, and others. Tiring of Chicago, a trip to Memphis in '59 followed. Then, in 1861, he returned to Chicago. In the same year, he became connected with the Chicago City Railway Company, and, during his service there, invented the improved one-horse cars. He was elected to his position in 1873, on an Independent ticket.

Throughout his varied experiences, Mr. Phillips can substantiate the appreciation of his friends by several substantial testimonials.

ALBERT PATCH.

This gentleman is the Assessor of the North Town of Chicago. He has been elected three times, the last by the votes of not only Republicans but of Democrats. In fact, if it were not for the votes of his Democratic friends, it is the general opinion he would not be elected.

The Assessor was born in Worcester, Massachusetts, in 1827, and thence went at the age of 19, to Haverill, Mass., where he engaged in the business of polishing pianos and other furniture, for the space of five years, in which he was an eminent success. Hence he went to Lawrence, Mass., and engaged in an unsuccessful dry goods business. He then came to Chicago, and resumed his former occupation. In 1856, he went to St. Louis, where he stayed for about four years. Now he returned to Chicago, and continued in the polishing business, which, becoming dull — to use his own words — he engaged in the butter business, and *slipped up* on it. He then went into the real estate business, in which he is at present engaged.

A. L. AMBERG.

The Assessor for the West Town of Chicago is Adam L. Amberg. This gentleman was born in New Jersey, May 22, 1841, but recollects very few experiences connected with his native place, from the fact that he left there when one year old to come (in company with his parents) to Chicago. The public life of Mr. Amberg is not a very extensive one. It was not before 1869 that he aspired to public emolument. In this year, he was appointed Clerk of the West Side Police Court, on the Citizens' ticket. He was subsequently re-appointed on the Fire-proof ticket. His conduct during both terms was such as to commend him to the people's suffrages for the position of West Town Assessor, to which he was elected in April, 1873.

Common Council.

WILLIAM H. RICHARDSON.

For a gentleman of 34, Mr. Richardson, one of the Aldermen, representing the First Ward, has seen experience in juristic matters not often witnessed. It is probably a fact that there is no lawyer who prosecutes a more extensive criminal business of a respectable character in the county than he. The matter is quite inevitable from the fact that, almost ever since he has begun practice, he has been associated with such men as Judge Knox, Carlos Haven, and Charles H. Reed. With the last-named, the Alderman, for a number of years, was in partnership. About the year 1870, Mr. Reed assuming the robes of the State's Attorney, the partnership was dissolved. Mr. Richardson has conducted practice alone ever since.

The Alderman was born near Buffalo, in 1840. In 1857, he went to Andover, Massachusetts, where he proceeded through a preparatory curriculum. About the year 1861, he came to Chicago, and read law, first with Judge Knox, and subsequently with other prominent lawyers. In 1872, he was elected Alderman of the First Ward on the "Law and Order" ticket. He vanquished a strong man when he worsted Mr. Philip Conley.

THOMAS FOLEY.

Certainly, Mr. Foley, the billiard king, is a self-made man ;
having spent just three months in school; and since then he
has been struggling against difficulties which to another man
would seem insurmountable.

Mr. Foley was born in Cashel, county of Tipperary, Ireland, August 16, 1842. In the fall of '49 he went to New
York. Here he stayed for about five years. At the early
age of twelve he came to Chicago, and became employed
brushing billiard tables in the old Tremont House. In 1860
he went to the Briggs House, and took charge of the bar.
Here he remained until 1865, when, importuned, he went to
Milwaukee and took charge of billiardistic matters in the
well known Newhall House. Tiring of this, he came back
to Chicago and engaged in business for himself, at the cor-
der of Dearborn and Monroe streets. Thence he removed
to his old, good-natured stand opposite the Post-office,
where others had failed repeatedly. Mr. Foley's friends
delight in calling attention to the fact, as an evidence of his
sterling popularity. In this locality Mr. Foley stayed up to
the fire. To recount the scenes witnessed there among the
greatest billiard artists in the world, would be nonsense.
Everybody has heard of " Tom. Foley." Poor John McDevitt
had just left there the night of the great fire, before he was
burned, and never found,

The fire wrought strange wonders with " Tom." Bracing
himself up, nevertheless, Mr. Foley went over to the West

Side, and leased for $1,500 — he did not have a cent, to the contrary, notwithstanding — a basement under the Barnes House; and, at the same time, started a place on Wabash avenue, near Twenty-Second street. Subsequently he leased his present place, fitted it up at the expense of $35,000, and made the grandest billiard palace in the world.

He was elected Alderman of the First Ward on the People's ticket, and congratulates himself on the fact that he is a first-class Irishman, and looks after one-fifth of the taxes of the entire city.

FRANCIS WHITAKER WARREN.

This gentleman represents the Second Ward, being elected in 1872, on the Republican ticket. He was placed in his position by a handsome majority.

He was born in the county of Sligo, Ireland, November 26, 1839, where he stayed until the age of twelve. Leaving his native place at this age, he proceeded to Boston, Mass., where he stayed five years, employed in the grocery trade. He then removed to Chicago, where he learned marble-cutting. He subsequently entered the livery business, in which he is at present engaged, doing a successful business.

In the Council, Alderman Warren acts on the Markets and Wharfing Privileges Committee. He is a "Law and Order" man, strictly speaking.

ARTHUR DIXON.

Alderman Dixon was elected to represent the Second Ward, in 1867, by a majority of 250; and in 1869, by a majority of 700.

He was born in Fermanaugh county, Ireland, in 1838, and when fifteen, came to Pittsburgh, Pennsylvania, and sandwiched an occasional tap on the farm. In 1860 he came to Chicago, and was engaged as a porter in a grocery store. He shortly after engaged in teaming, and prosecutes the same to-day on an extensive scale, giving all the time and attention demanded. He exactly knows the requirements, having handled the lines on every vehicle known to invention, from a dray up.

Politically, Alderman Dixon is considerable of a success. In 1869 he was elected to a position in the National Executive Committee, by the Irish Republican Convention, of which he is now Treasurer. In 1870 he was elected to the General Assembly. Here Alderman Dixon gained distinction by his efforts in the one mill tax matter on special assessments, and in the alleged Springfield clique question. He is also a member of the Republican Executive Committee, and a member of the Irish Literary Society.

14

DAVID COEY.

Elected from the Third Ward, on the Republican ticket, first in 1870 — 500 majority. The Alderman is about forty-six years of age. He was born of Scotch-Irish parents (Old School Presbyterian), near Belfast, Ireland, and, having attended a semi-theological seminary, took a sudden idea and a life partner, and left the romantic heath of his father, to grow wealthy in America, before he was twenty-one. He was all the time bent upon coming to Chicago, but went to New York first, that he might, by contrast, better in after days admire the inevitable growth of the western prairies. Here he pursued carpentry for a matter of six years, when he came to Chicago (in 1852).

Resuming his trade, he drifted gradually into the building business on his own account, to suffer in the '57 crisis. The number of structures he has erected since, intimate that his disaster was not permanent.

The Alderman is fervent on retrenchment. For a quiet man he created considerable excitement by changing his vote when the appropriation for Union Park came up. He changed his vote at 11:45, P. M., and caused the defeat of the entire appropriation bill.

WILLIAM FITZGERALD.

Ald. Fitzgerald was elected on the People's ticket in 1873 to represent the Third Ward — a district said to contain the largest number of colored residents in the city. His majority over the other two candidates in the field was about 480.

The Alderman was born in Coachford, County of Cork, Ireland, a little west of the City of Cork, in 1842. In 1850, he came to Skaneateles, New York, where he stayed until 1858. In this year, he went to Seneca Falls, N. Y., and acquired a knowledge of the tin trade. Having traveled through nearly all of the Western States, he finally came to Chicago, and in 1865 made it his permanent home. It was not long before the alderman, realizing the vast promise of trade, established himself in the hardware business at 589 State Street, where he is still located. He also started a flourishing branch store at 107 Blue Island Avenue. The fruits of his business enterprise are visible in several substantial buildings, among them the Fifth Avenue Hotel — a structure 92 x 41, and containing 78 rooms.

The Alderman is and always has been a Democrat. Public emolument seems to be an acquisition he never coveted much. In fact, he had been offered an aldermanship twice, and refused the office. He stands upon the Committee on Printing, and is Chairman of the Committee on Local Assessments.

JESSE SPALDING.

This gentleman represents the Fourth Ward. He was elected in 1873, on the Republican ticket. This is about the only political position he has filled, not devoting much attention to public honors.

Mr. Spalding was born in Pennsylvania, and is about 45 years of age. He is a member of the Menominee River Lumber Company, and is a very extensive owner of Michigan pine lands. His colleague is George H. Sidwell.

A. H. PICKERING.

Aquila Herford Pickering was elected to represent the Fifth Ward on an Independent Ticket, by a majority of about 1,400. Ex-Alderman Peter Daggy was one of his two opponents. The Alderman was born on a farm on Short Creek, Harrison county, Ohio, near Cadiz, the county-seat, in 1820. At the age of 14, he was placed at school, and remained under careful tuition until arrived at the age of 21. In 1841, he went to Salem, Henry county, Iowa, and in that locality pursued a thriving mercantile business, under the name and style of "Pickering's Emporium." Here he remained until 1863. In this year he came to Chicago, and engaged in general commission business, and the salt trade. The latter he abandoned in 1871, and gave his exclusive attention to grain. In this trade he has been, and is to-day, one of the very heaviest operators in the market.

In the Council, Alderman Pickering was the first to move for a new franchise for the Gas Company, but was defeated. One of his best movements was the introduction of an ordinance for the prevention of cruelty to animals. He was also the originator of the idea of putting iron-pipes into lofty buildings for the use of the Fire Department; although the credit was given to ex-Mayor Medill. His mind is at present filled with the propriety of selling the Lake front at a fair valuation.

RICHARD B. STONE.

This gentleman represents, in the Common'Council, the Fifth Ward. He ·was elected in Nòvember, 1871, on the Fire-Proof ticket, by a .majority of 397. He was elected in 1873 on the Citizen's Union ticket, by a majority of 867; the whole number of votes given to his opponent, only approximating 938.

The Alderman was born in Oxford, Worcester county, Massachusetts, in 1829. At the age of six, he went to Bridgewater, in Plymouth county, Massachusetts. He then went as an apprentice to the carpenter trade, and attached himself to the business until 1851. He subsequently went to Western New York, and bought an interest in a sash factory and lumber business. In 1855, losing his health, he went to a water-cure in the east. On April 19, 1856, he came to Chicago. Here he entered the lumber business, and is still engaged in it.

During his first term in the Council he served with distinction on the Committees on Bridewell, Streets and Alleys, and Printing. During his second term, he served on the Bridewell, Streets and Alleys, and County Relations Committees. He was a strict supporter of the measures advocated by the " Law and Order " men.

ALDERMAN SCHMITZ.

This gentleman represents the Sixth Ward, having been re-elected, in 1872, on the Republican ticket. In his election, on each occasion, almost the stoutest support he has received has come from the Democrats. He is forty-five years of age.

He was born in the province of the Rhine, Prussia, and served in carpentry up to 1850. At this time, as provided by the enactments of his country, he joined the army. He had only served two years, when his services bore him into the Sergeantcy. In 1855 the Alderman came to Chicago; and in 1857 commenced business as a builder, in which he is now engaged. During his second term in the Council, Alderman Schmitz followed up the record of his previous term, by looking devotedly after the matter of sewerage and water service. Among other projects, he rigidly conserved the people's interest against railroad intrusion; was an ardent abater of slaughter-house nuisances; and fought hard for the banishment of Healy Slough.

PHILLIP REIDY.

This gentleman represents the Sixth Ward, elected on the People's ticket by a very large majority; three other candidates being in the field. The confidence Mr. Reidy has won among his constituents he secured only after a long career of untiring industry in their midst.

The Alderman was born in Tralee, county of Kerry, Ireland, in 1831, and, at the age of twenty-two, proceeded to New York. In February, 1854, he came to Chicago, and adopted blacksmithing, locating at the canal locks, in Bridgeport, in 1856. In this business he is still engaged; having accumulated therein considerable of a competence.

In the Council Mr. Reidy favors the least possible display in the sale of liquors on Sunday. He serves on the Committee on Schools, Licenses, and Local Assessments. He is also the President of St. Vincent's Society, of St. Bridget's church; and of the Hibernian Benevolent Society; manifesting much interest in church organization.

PATRICK McCLORY.

This gentleman was elected from the Seventh Ward, on the Republican ticket, in 1872, by a large majority. The influence of the Personal Liberty League conspicuously manifested itself on the occasion.

Alderman McClory was born in the county of Down, Ireland, in 1831. At the age of eighteen, the Alderman, exhibiting an unmistakable inclination to see everything worth seeing throughout the world, by an expressed wish to go to New Zealand, his father attempted to place him on the constabulary force. He was too young, however. At the age of nineteen his predilection to travel finally culminated in a trip to Glasgow, in Scotland. He remained here about two years, employed at the trade of boiler making in a large ship building establishment. He then returned to Ireland, but did not stay longer than about a year, when he set out for Liverpool with a one-pound note. Here he obtained employment in Baring & Bros.' warehouse. Finding matters in this part of the world distasteful, he finally came to America, working his passage for $12.50, and arriving in New York, with one shilling and sixpence. He soon procured a position, as all competent workmen do; firstly in the Novelty Iron Works; then with the great Manhattan Gas Company; and afterward assisted at the construction of the Metropolitan Gas Works. For three years subsequently he acted as foreman of the gas works in Troy, New York. Removing to Chicago, the Alderman connected himself with the People's Gas Light and Coke Company, where he is at the present writing.

E. F. CULLERTON.

This gentleman represents the Seventh Ward in the Council. He was born in Chicago, in 1842, and devoted his early life to a rigid public school education. At the age of 19 he struck out for himself, and built, in a very short time, a rushing boarding-house and livery-stable business.

In 1871, he was elected by a very large majority to represent the Seventh Ward. In 1872 he was elected to the Legislature. Here he distinguished himself in opposition to the West Side Park Commissioners' taxation scheme. In the Council he occupies a high position on gas and police matters. He was re-elected on the People's ticket.

The record of Alderman Cullerton in the Common Council is a very satisfactory one to his constituents. No vital question, as well in a general sense, escapes his closest attention.

The alderman rarely speaks. When he does, his speech is the result of the most thorough conviction.

M. B. BAILEY.

This gentleman represents the Eighth Ward. He was elected in 1870 on the Republican ticket, though an old Democrat, and in 1872 on the People's ticket. His first term in the Council was noted by his herculean efforts to promote the sewerage facilities of his ward, securing the same when no appropriation had been made. A prominent feature of his second term was his minority report on the Tilly plan for a new Court House. He also distinguished himself by his efforts for the Canal and Twelfth street viaducts. The Alderman was born in Limerick — near the boundaries — Ireland, in 1837, the year in which Chicago was incorporated. About the age of 16 he came to Chicago and acquired the mason and plastering art. In 1855 he went into business for himself, taking every contract he could get. In the latter part of 1856, setting forth from Lawrence, Kansas, he went to the Rocky Mountains, and after six months came back to St. Joseph, Missouri, where he built several large structures.

He then came to Chicago, where many a foot of land bears the weight of his work. Among many other structures, he has built the new County Jail, the Second National Bank, the Empire Block, the Washington School, Father Waldron's School, Schœllkopf's, on Randolph street, and Cohn Brother's Building. The Alderman's ambition is building.

JAMES H. HILDRETH.

This is the second term of Alderman James Henry Hildreth, in the Common Council, having been elected first in 1869 to represent the Seventh Ward, and in 1873, on the People's ticket, to represent the Eighth. The districts are almost identical, the numbers of the Wards being changed by the Legislature.

Mr. Hildreth was born in Chester county, Massachusetts, July 8, 1840, and is of American descent. At about the age of 19, having spent a short time farming in Will county, he came to Chicago, procuring, upon his arrival, a conductorship from the North Side City Railway Company. This position he subsequently abandoned for an appointment as Grain Inspector under the Board of Trade. In 1862, upon the organization of the Board of Trade Battery, our subject enlisted and proceeded to the front. In all of the principal battles fought by this deservedly famous organization, Mr. Hildreth took a prominent part; remembering the stirring incidents of no less than 34 battles, and the capture of the head and front of the Southern Confederacy, Jefferson Davis. The army life of the Alderman is replete in a continuous series of thrilling adventures which well illustrate the daring spirit of the man. On one occasion, in the vicinity of Covington, Georgia, a few horses of the division giving very good promise of dropping under their riders, Hildreth was dispatched, as he always was on such occasions, to look about for substitutes. He had not gone far before he met with the most brilliant success. It was so encouraging, in fact, as to keep him so long absent that his companions gave him up for dead. While ruminating over his untimely demise, the boys were suddenly aroused by the appearance of a batch of horses and mules, numbering in all 27, and commanded by negroes. Four horsemen bringing up the rear comprised Corporal Hildreth, a Rebel lieutenant-colonel, and two privates. The animals were bagged while hotly pursued into apparent safety, by the negroes; the officer was surprised from the shadow of a tree; and the two privates were captured when half way through a fence, having just bidden an affectionate farewell to their sweethearts. In recognition of his extraordinary service on this occasion, he was presented with a magnificent testimonial. On his return from the war, Mr. Hildreth received his old position on the Board of Trade.

The trying scenes of the Great Fire counted no bolder hero than Hildreth. As very often happens, however, the glory of his achievements was appropriated to the credit of somebody else. When the water supply had ceased, bringing panic into the hearts of the bravest, Hildreth, with the suddenness of thought, hurried to the powder magazines on South Water street, near State, and, bursting the doors open, gathered up all of the kegs of powder and fuse he could find, and, through showers of sparks and clouds of suffocating smoke, proceeded to the work of blowing-up. The first building that trembled was the Union National Bank; then Smith & Nixon's. In his experience in these structures, Mr. Hildreth learned that he did not succeed as well as he might. The subsequent efforts of the Alderman proved more successful, the following buildings tumbling above the powder with tremendous beauty: at the northwest and southwest corners of Washington street and Wabash avenue; at the corner of State and Harrison, where the fire was

checked; and about six buildings on the north side of Congress street, near Wabash avenue.   Yet, the wires flashed in
all directions the news of the perilous powder performance
entirely credited to Gen. Phil. Sheridan.   This mistake,
however, might arise from the fact that Police Commisioner
Sheridan took a prominent part in the proceeding, and that
Gen. Sheridan was present in the burning city.

JAMES O'BRIEN.

This gentleman was elected by a very large majority to represent the Ninth Ward in the Common Council. Votes to the number of 1,025 in this ward is something to be proud of.

The Alderman was born in the county of Wexford, Ireland, July 25, 1842. His early life was not replete in anything very extraordinary. Before his advent in Chicago, in fact, nothing occurred, it may be said, to mar the harmony of a very ordinary life. Railroad enterprise had fascinations for him, and commencing at car coupling, he, in a brief time, was appointed assistant yard-master in the employ of the Michigan Southern. Relinquishing this business after a time, he entered the retail liquor business, in which he is now engaged.

In the Council Alderman O'Brien's position is a peculiar, but doughty one. He has convictions, and insists always upon vindicating them. It is true, he generally stands in the minority; but his status is, to say the least, very manly. He stood against the confirmation of Commissioners Wright and Mason, as a matter of law; and in the slate made by Mayor Colvin, was the first Alderman to exercise the spirit of his independence.

THOMAS F. BAILEY.

Thomas Francis Bailey was elected from the Ninth Ward in 1873, on the People's ticket, by a majority of about 470. One of his opponents was Ex-Alderman Powell, whose strength in the ward was very great.

Alderman Bailey was born in Lough Gur, Limerick, in 1842. He is, therefore, 32 years of age. He remained in his native place perhaps until arrived at the age of 11. He then went to Bradford county, Pennsylvania, and worked on a farm. In 1856, having reconsidered an intention to settle in Michigan, he came to Chicago, and entered general merchandise, serving in Shufeldt's distillery as general foreman up to Jan. 1, 1874.

The election of Alderman Bailey from so peculiar a ward as the Ninth, it is said, even surprised himself only less than it did Ex-Alderman Powell.

DAVID W. CLARK, Jr.

This gentleman is Alderman of the Tenth Ward, having defeated C. C. P. Holden, Esq., in 1872, on the straight Republican ticket. He had not the remotest idea of achieving the victory, as it was generally supposed Mr. Holden could not be beaten in a ward he had represented so long.

Mr. Clark was born in Boston, Massachusetts, May 6, 1840. In 1853, he left there and proceeded to New York, where he stayed one year. He then came to Chicago and entered the job printing business, in which he is now engaged. He was Supervisor in 1871, representing the Tenth Ward, and through his exertions principally, it is claimed, the abstract matter was referred to the incoming Board, whereby the county, it is estimated, was saved $1,250,000.

In the earlier life of our subject he figured well in the Volunteer Fire Department, receiving a medal in 1859, on Company 2 of the Fire Brigade, for not missing an alarm or fire during the year. In the same year he was elected First Lieutenant of the Company. He also served in Barker's Dragoons during the war. This company formed Gen. McClellan's body guard through West Virginia. Mr. Clark was Secretary of W. B. Warren Lodge of the Masonic order, and in 1868 received a magnificent gold watch and chain for meritorious services.

15

C. L. WOODMAN.

Charles Leonard Woodman represents the Tenth Ward in the Common Council, elected in 1873 on the "Law and Order" ticket, by about 700 majority. This is the Alderman's fourth term in the Common Council. He represented, under the administration of Mayor Sherman, the Eighth Ward; represented the Sixteenth Ward on Sherman's second term, and was elected from the Twentieth Ward after the Great Fire. In this connection it may be interesting to state that, when chosen to represent the Twentieth Ward, there was scarcely a house there to relieve the monotony of a prairie waste. The old residents were compelled to travel from their scattered habitations throughout the city to be represented in a ward they did not live in. The contests in the Council Alderman Woodman remembers with pleasure, concern the improvement of the mouth of the river, the construction of the great Lake Tunnel, and the deepening of the Chicago River. All of these he successfully favored against active opposition. He was also most conspicuous on the Railroad Committee.

Mr. Woodman was born in Barrington, Stafford County, N. H., July 7, 1829. At the age of thirteen, he removed to Great Falls, and, excepting six months at school, devoted himself to the bakery business, in company with his brother. In those days no machinery being at hand, it occupied the time of four men and a boy to turn one barrel of flour into crackers. Now, one man can work five barrels per day.

At the age of twenty, Mr. Woodman built an oven in Great Falls, and went into business for himself. After the lapse of five years, he came to Chicago. Immediately upon arrival, he secured a position at fifteen dollars per week, competent workmen receiving at the time from six to eight dollars. His position was the superintendency of a bakery at the corner of Dearborn and Illinois streets. He soon bought this establishment out, and did well enough to start a more extensive business on the South Side. Forming a copartnership with Joseph M. Dake,— now dead,— he established himself on Dearborn street, near the Post-office, where his shingle was visible at the time of the Fire. It was here he conceived the " aerated bread " idea, which was so popular for a time. About five years ago, in company with Edward Olcott, he built a bakery on Kinzie street. Both of his establishments, as well as his residence, were burned in the great Fire, entailing a loss of about $75,000. The loss did not affect the spirit of the Alderman much, however. Within thirty days after the fire, he was baking one hundred barrels a day in his temporary structure, on the corner of Adams and Canal streets. The extent of his business since can be judged from the following, taken from his ledger: For 1873, upwards of 30,000 barrels of flour made into bread and crackers — production, 1,500,000 loaves of bread, and 75,000 barrels of crackers. Sales, over $125,000 more than previous year.

PATRICK KEHOE.

Patrick Kehoe was elected to represent the Eleventh Ward, in 1872, on the People's ticket, by a most favorable majority.

Mr. Kehoe was born in Carlow County, in the town of Clonegall, Ireland, in 1834. In 1854, he came to Chicago, and established a flourishing grocery business in the vicinity of his present locality, corner of Carroll and Halsted streets. It was in an era in Chicago's history when a little foresight would work tremendous marvels for a man. That commodity forming one of our subject's capabilities, he succeeded in building himself up remarkably fast.

Mr. Kehoe has not figured very prominently in politics, devoting most scrupulous attention to trade.

GEORGE E. WHITE.

This gentleman represents the Eleventh Ward. He was elected in 1873, on the People's ticket, and is the youngest man in the Council, and one of the shrewdest. He was born in Millbury, Massachusetts, in 1848, and left there at the age of 13, to graduate in North Wilberham College, About 15 he entered the army.

In the battles for the Union, Alderman White took a prominent part, figuring in no less than 17 battles. Among other reminiscences, he was present at Lee's surrender. He fought under Meade, Burnside, and Wilcox, and was three times wounded. At the beginning of the war, he went out under Col. Bartlett, now Brevet Major General, a bosom friend, and a magnificent officer.

At the end of the war, Alderman White settled in Chicago, working for Messrs. White & Ellson at a salary of $50 per month. He then went into business for himself, when the firm name was Burchard, White & Co. Burchard was now bought out, and the firm name was White & Haffner. Mr. White now bought out Haffner, and ran the lumber business himself; in which he is now engaged.

The extent of the Alderman's business may be learned from the fact that his pay-roll per week amounts to $2,000. His acquaintances say he is worth $75,000.

AMOS F. MINER.

Amos F. Miner was elected to represent the Twelfth Ward in the Common Council, in 1872, on the Republican ticket, by a majority of about 386 ; two other candidates being in the field.

The Alderman was born in Grafton county, New Hampshire, in 1826. At the age of eight he left his native place and went to Rensselaer county, New York, where he went to work on a farm; devoting his leisure hours to the acquisition of an education. He then became a school teacher. But the birch and rule did not develop sufficient muscle to wield, very healthily, the hammer of life. Accordingly the Alderman learned the carpenter's and joiner's trade. Having acquired a thorough knowledge of the business, he proceeded to Westchester county, where he remained three or four years. He then removed to Desplaines, Cook county, Illinois, where he remained for about ten years. In both of these places he was quite busily engaged in building enterprises. He has been since, and is now, engaged in building.

Ten years ago Mr. Miner was admitted to the Bar, but did not enter practice. He has interested himself in public affairs for some time; yet he does not care to figure much politically, it seems. Among other positions of public trust he served as Assistant Examiner of Schools in the Northwest, under Greenleaf, and as a Justice of the Peace for five years. He came to Chicago in 1866.

MONROE HEATH.

Monroe Heath, Alderman of the Twelfth Ward, was re-elected in the fall of 1873, on the "Law and Order" ticket, by about 986 majority. Only seventeen votes stood against him on his first election on the Fire-Proof ticket.

Mr. Heath was born in Springfield, Sullivan county, New Hampshire, in 1828. His ancestors, on the maternal side, it is pretty clearly established, came over in the Mayflower; and the very fair presumption is that his progenitors were of English descent.

His mother dying when our subject was but four years old, and his father when he was but eight, circumstances required the placing of the boy in the custody of his grandmother. The old lady took care of him up to the age of about seventeen. He now went to Boston, and acquired a knowledge of general merchandise. Henceforward, up to his arrival in Chicago, his mercantile career was relieved by considerable traveling; experience in the Mexican war, and a trip to Pike's Peak, contributing enlivening reminiscences.

In the early part of 1851 Mr. Heath came to Chicago, when he immediately engaged in the painting business. The first locality he selected was upon the North Side, in the vicinity of Wells street bridge. During the first year he employed but four or five men. In the second year the force was increased to about forty. He then removed to the South Side, and, in company with Mr. Henry Milligan, with whom he associated in 1855, has since succeeded in building up the magnificent proportions of business they now enjoy, on East Randolph street, near LaSalle. To go into detail regarding the immense progress made by the firm of Heath & Milligan since its organization, would be superfluous. The entire business community built up in Chicago recognize Messrs. Heath & Milligan as standing at the very head and front of the most successful in their particular line of business.

Their success they have achieved, too, under quite discouraging circumstances. The firm was burned out twice, and lost heavily. They rebuilt immediately after the first occasion, and after the second. The latter occasion happened to be that of the great fire, an event distinctly remembered, it is presumed. The present establishment they entered about ninety days after the great disaster.

AVERY MOORE.

This gentleman represents the Thirteenth Ward in the Common Council, elected on the Republican ticket, in 1872. He was elected first in 1865, from the old Seventh Ward, being, it is said, the first Republican ever elected in that district.

Mr. Moore was born in Belmont county, Ohio, in 1830. Here he remained up to the age of 25, devoting his days to school and a mercantile career. He now removed to Warsaw, Hancock county, Illinois, where he taught school and pursued real estate principally. In 1863 — after having constructed a commendable war record — Mr. Moore came to Chicago. In 1864, he entered the employ of the Chicago, Burlington, & Quincy Railroad. He subsequently left this institution and established himself in the storage business, corner of Rush and Kinzie streets.

Mr. Moore's first political experience was in Ohio, where he represented Belmont county in convention. Among other positions of trust, Mr. Moore has served honorably in the Board of Education.

J. L. CAMPBELL.

Alderman Campbell was first elected in 1869, from the Thirteenth Ward, on the straight Republican ticket, by a majority of 262.

He was born in Livingston county, New York, and came to Illinois at the age of 19, settling in Elgin. After a stay of six years in the milk (and water) region, Alderman Camp bell went to Northern Iowa, and studied in the Iowa University, in Lafayette. Since that time his progress in his (legal) profession has been very rapid. The political promi nence of Alderman Campbell was first made manifest in *Idaho, when the question was first agitated of organizing a territory east of the mountains. He went to Washington at this time, and stayed there until the territory known as Montana had been an accomplished fact. He is responsible for the events that conspired to effect it. The fact was duly appreciated by the denizens of that locality, Alderman Campbell having been invited to represent the people of that region in Congress immediately. Having accepted the merited honor, he was on his way thither, when a horde of Indians between Fort Kearney and Denver intercepted his approach. The event checked the political aspirations of the Alderman, but not much. Subsequent history stands as evidence of the fact.

BARTHOLOMEW QUIRK.

The Alderman, representing the Fourteenth Ward, was elected on the Republican ticket, in 1872. He was born in Castle Gregory, County of Kerry, Ireland, in 1834. In 1841 he went to Albany, New York; thence to Buffalo; and, in 1844, came to Chicago.

He spent about four years in school, firstly in the old Planter's House, and afterwards at the Old Dearborn. He now went to printing. His employer failing to pay, the Alderman failed to make pi, etc., and went to carpentry. He remained in the business to become a successful builder of residences. The Alderman was for three years and three months in the army, serving in the Twenty-Third Illinois. In the principle battles shared by that regiment, Mr. Quirk participated. He accompanied Mulligan, Sheridan and Cook through all of the engagements, mostly in Western Virginia; witnessed "Sheridan's ride," and was within fifty feet of Colonel Mulligan when killed.

SILAS E. CLEVELAND.

This gentleman represents the Fourteenth Ward, and has been elected twice: in 1871, on the Fire-Proof ticket; and in 1873, on the "Law and Order" ticket. He was born in Clinton county, New York, in 1839. In 1849 the family removed to Chicago, and placed the Alderman at school; first at Hathaway's old school, then at Washington school, and also at Mount Morris College, Ogle county, Illinois. He then went to work in the carpenter shop of his father, spending a short time with Olmstead & Nickerson, architects. He was soon placed in the carpenter shop, in charge of the planing department. In 1861 he accompanied his father, a captain in the Eighth Illinois cavalry, to the front; and witnessed, among other battles, the fight in front of Richmond, and the battles of Bull Run, Malvern Hill, and Williamsburg. In 1862 he filled several building contracts with the Pittsburg & Ft. Wayne Road. He also served three years as a mail agent on the Northwestern Road. Since then he has been engaged in prosperous business enterprises.

In the Council the Alderman favors strongly the principle of the "Law and Order" party, and advocated fervently the closing of the saloons on Sunday.

NICHOLAS ECKHARDT.

Mr. Eckhardt is Alderman of the Fifteenth Ward, and was elected in 1872 on an Independent ticket, by a majority of 156, two other candidates being in the field.

He was born in 1832 in Germany, and left his native country at the age of 17. He then came almost directly to Chicago. Here he learned the carpentry trade, and relieved the monotony of his avocation by running, like so many citizens, in the Fire Department. He was on the regular Fire Department for eight years, serving as pipeman on the "Queen," and subsequently on the "Brown." He is at present engaged in the liquor trade.

J. J. McGRATH.

Alderman McGrath represents the Fifteenth Ward in the Common Council.

Born in Ireland, he came, when quite young, to America, and settled with an uncle in New York City, where he received a liberal education. He then learned cooperage, transacting the same for several years, and finally became interested in the Chicago Distilling Company. He was shortly appointed superintendent over some eighty men, then employed in the business of cooperage. He subsequently purchased the institution, and now employs about fifty operatives.

He visited Canada, and the Southern States, returned to his native land in 1867, glanced at the principal cities of the Old World, and dropped in to view the marvels of industry in the Paris Exposition. It was on this trip Alderman McGrath acquired the extensive knowledge he has so often displayed in sewerage, water supplies, and kindred subjects of municipal importance. When the sewer bill of Corporation Counsel Tuley was pending before the body, the report submitted on the question by Alderman McGrath, Chairman of the Sewer Committee, will be recalled as a document of a most exhaustive nature.

PETER MAHR.

Alderman Peter Mahr was elected to represent the Six-teenth Ward, on the Republican ticket, in 1872. He was born in Nassau, Germany, June 11, 1835, and lived under the paternal roof up to the age of 15. While the old people were doing very well in Fatherland, they thought, neverthe-less, that their heir might grow more useful to himself in America. With this intention, the family removed to this country and settled down to agricultural pursuits in Wis-consin. Their stay was but short. The golden grain was very pretty, indeed, in the eyes of Peter, but the suggestions it afforded were more practical than poetic. The result of his education was that he became a brewer. He pursued this avocation in Wisconsin until he thought it would pay better in Illinois.

He accordingly came to Chicago, and gave his services to Lill & Diversy for many years. He then went into business for himself. He was elected a Ward Supervisor for two years, and a Town Supervisor for about the same period.

THOMAS W. STOUT.

Alderman Thomas W. Stout was elected to represent the Sixteenth Ward in 1871 on the Star Chamber, and in 1873 on the People's ticket. He was born in Pennsylvania, Sept. 15, 1836. The early education of the Alderman assisted his fondness for a mercantile life materially. In several fields of industry his work has made a very perceptible impress ; securing, as he did, a position in the employ of the North-western Railway Company, that gave him ample opportunities. He held a position on this road for no less than 22 years.

In the Council he was a strenuous advocate of closing saloons on Sundays up to 1 p. m. ; conspicuously figuring on the Committee of Nine. He was a strong opposer of gas monopoly ; having advocated a measure which he claims would save the city the sum of $200,000 annually.

LOUIS SCHAFFNER.

Alderman Schaffner, better known as Col. Schaffner, represents the Seventeenth Ward.

He was born in Alsace, France, and is now 46 years of age. At the age of nine, Col. Schaffner removed to the city of New York, and engaged in the dry goods business, where he remained until the outbreak of the Rebellion, when he organized, Jan. 8, 1861, Company A, of the Seventh New York Volunteers (Steuben). Elected Captain, the Colonel assumed, very modestly, however, the rank of Adjutant, confiding in future merit for a soldier's promotion, and winning it bravely. Col. Schaffner participated in the fight at Big Bethel, at Ball's Bluff, and Port Hudson, and many other engagements, and suffered, during his service through the entire war, two severe sunstrokes, and but a slight wound in the knee, which he received when Lieutenant Grebel was killed beside him. Promoted to the Lieutenant Colonelcy in a short time after the commencement of the struggle, he subsequently declined two offers of a brevet Brigadier-Generalship. He had also charge of the prisoners at Rock Island and Camp Douglas. In the dawn of peace he entered the grocery business, and left it for the office of Assistant Assessor of Internal Revenue.

In 1868, Col. Schaffner, always a staunch Republican, handled the North Side Tanners so well that every ward in the Division went Republican at the Presidential election. In 1869, he was defeated, but in 1870, he was elected to a seat in the Council by a handsome majority.

16

JACOB LENGACHER.

This gentleman was elected to represent the Seventeenth Ward in the Common Council. First time in 1871, on the Union People's ticket; the second time in 1873, on the People's ticket.

He was born in Berne, Switzerland, in 1833. One year and a half at school in Berne, and up to 1858, in the city of Deintigen, completed his educational course. He now came to Laporte, Indiana. He here entered into a contract for clearing land five miles or so distant from the city of Laporte. He subsequently entered the brewing business. In August, 1861, with some fourteen friends, the Alderman proceeded to Indianapolis, and offered his services to Gen. Willich, commander of the 32d Indiana. Promotion soon succeeded. Corporalship, sergeantcy, lieutenantships, and captaincy followed. After the battle of Shiloh, he was compelled to take an orderly sergeantship. When the Captain of Company D was killed, the Alderman, who belonged to Company I, was appointed to his position.

Coming to Chicago, he entered the Collector's office. Business growing dull, however, he went, at suggestion, into the insurance business, in which he is now engaged. He represents eight different companies.

THOMAS CANNON.

This gentleman represents the Eighteenth Ward in the Common Council. He was born in the townland of Clooncoe, County Leitrim, Ireland, May 15, 1828, and came to this country in 1851, coming directly to Chicago. Up-hill work encountered the Alderman at once. He succeeded in obtaining employment, however, very soon, as a laborer, from which he rose to a position as forwarding freight agent for the old Galena Railroad. After six years of dilligent service here, Mr. Cannon was removed to make place for the pet of certain politicians. The Alderman had accumulated considerable money in the meantime, and this he invested in real estate. He had hardly done so, however, when the financial crash of '58 and '59 swept it away. Then followed a checkered career. Firstly he speculated on the Board of Trade; had bad luck, after seven years, and went to teaming; was then engaged as a Sidewalk Inspector, under the Board of Public Works; then as an United States Mail Agent. He now procured a position in the Custom House, whence he was discharged, with twenty others, for want of employment. But the Alderman had made friends. Governor Beveridge was one of them. At the demise of Owen Dougherty, Mr. Cannon was appointed by his Excellency to fill the vacancy as a Justice of the Peace, which position he now holds. His successful race for Alderman was his third: in the first heat being beaten by five hundred and seventy-four majority; in the second, by twenty-seven; and being successful in the last by a majority of five hundred and sixty-four. The Alderman prides himself upon having built the first house on the North Side after the great fire.

DAVID MURPHY.

This gentleman represents the Eighteenth Ward in the Common Council, and was elected in 1873, on the People's ticket. He was born in the county of Wexford, Ireland; and, leaving there twenty years ago, came directly to Chicago.

The experience of the Alderman in a business point of view—for he was never much in politics—deserves more than a passing notice. On his arrival in Chicago he went into partnership with his brother, Collector Murphy, in the grocery business, and has been ever since invariably successful.

In politics, Mr. Murphy, as before intimated, did but little. However, having been pressed upon by his friends, he accepted a candidacy, and won the Aldermanship of the Eighteenth Ward, by a majority of four hundred and one, three other candidates being in the field. He ran against Ex-Alderman Carney before, but was defeated.

In the Council Mr. Murphy is quite conservative; catering to the senses of no other representative, but closely watching the interests of his ward. His constituents appreciate the fact.

MICHAEL BRAND.

Elected to represent the Nineteenth Ward in the Common Council, Mr. Brand took his seat as the result of the fall election, in 1873.

The gentleman established a brewing business at 30 Cedar street, he may well feel proud of, years ago, and in establishing the same has carefully eschewed politics.

THOMAS LYNCH.

The colleague of Alderman Brand is Thomas Lynch, elected by a handsome majority to represent the district in which he lives.

The utmost confidence is reposed by his constituents in Alderman Lynch, and the prospects are that he will not betray it.

JOHN T. CORCORAN.

Mr. Corcoran was elected to represent the Twentieth Ward, in 1872, on the Greeley ticket, by a majority of about 900; two other candidates being in the field. One received 98 votes; the other 180. The Alderman was born in Killarney, and is 37 years of age. When but five weeks old, he was removed by his parents to the city of Ottawa, Ontario. Here the family stayed for about eight years. They now came to Chicago. In those days there were not so many hotels in Chicago as now. They were not so ornate, besides, what there were of them. The old St. Louis, however, was about as respectable as any of them. This edifice Mr. Corcoran's father purchased, and succeeded in establishing in a very brief time. The hotel stood on East Washington street, near Franklin, and was subsequently burned. The father dying in 1854, a rather flourishing grocery business and the care of six young children devolved upon the Alderman. He did not prosecute the business very long, as he saw something more lucrative in hotel life. He accordingly secured the old Continental, a building with 35 rooms. Here he laid the foundation of his subsequent success. This was about eleven years ago. Foreseeing even then the possibilities of trade, Mr. Corcoran advanced in close proximity to railroad travel, and purchased the Hatch House, located on the southeast corner of Fifth avenue and Kinzie street. From the outset the career of the house was brilliant; although street improvement took off considerable of the profit, the building of the Fifth avenue viaduct and the consequent elevation of the street costing the Alderman $22,400. The building had 118 rooms for guests at the time of the great fire. It was insured for $35,000, and of this the Alderman recovered perhaps 18½ per cent. The present building cost $17,000.

In the Council Alderman Corcoran, during the past year, has stood in the minority. He was bitterly opposed to the Mayor's bill as being tyrannical, and has the best hopes for the entire success of the People's party.

JULIUS JONAS.

Julius Jonas is the colleague of Alderman J. T. Corcoran, in the administration of the affairs of the Twentieth Ward. He was elected to his position in 1873.

It is the impression of the residents of the Twentieth Ward that Alderman Jonas will fulfill the requirements of his office with entire satisfaction.

Mr. Jonas was born in Pleshen, Prussia, and is 37 years of age. At the age of 14, he came to New York. After a stay here of about five years he went to Quincy, Illinois. He then came to Chicago, and opened the hide business, over 231 S. Water street, and subsequently removed to 183 Michigan street. His annual business here, added to that of several branches, approximates $800,000.

Mr. Jonas has not paid much attention to politics; giving deep attention to his business. As a result, he has succeeded in building up a remarkable business.

PART III.

COUNTY OFFICERS.

H. B. MILLER.

H. B. Miller is the County Treasurer, elected by the People's Party in the Fall of 1873 by a very large majority. When placed on the ticket, the opposition sought very hard to prove that he was not an American. Indeed, a large number of voters believed he was not, from his connection with the interests of our German residents. A sketch of his history, however, will show that, if ever a man could be Americanized, Mr. Miller enjoys that sweet boon with a vengeance.

H. B. Miller was born in 1819, in the Lebanon Valley, in Pennsylvania, where his great grandfather settled about the year 1720. Both of his grandfathers were born in America, and fought under Washington's banner in the struggle for national independence.

At the age of 14, he entered a printing office, learned the trade, and pursued it for four years, or thereabouts. In 1839, fast acquiring a taste for journalism, Mr. Miller founded, in Niles, Michigan, an English paper, the *Republican*, and edited it till 1844. In this year he founded the *Telegraph*, at Kalamazoo. Both of these journals — the latter advocating the principles of Henry Clay — he edited with much ability; and recognition of their political influence was not slow in making itself apparent.

In 1845, he removed to Buffalo. In this city he followed up his journalistic aspirations, and founded a German paper, the *Telegraph*, which is still in existence. Subsequently,

President Taylor appointed him Chief Inspector of the Lighthouses on the Lakes.

Severing his connection with the Press, Mr. Miller, after a time, became a contractor of Public Works. While so engaged, by order of the British-American Telegraph Company he constructed a telegraph line from Quebec to Montreal. Subsequently, he built a mile of the enlargement of the Erie Canal, and a dock and landing on the Niagara River for the Buffalo and Lake Huron Railroad, which cost about $1,500,000. In 1858, Buffalo elected him a member of the State Legislature, and the next year re-elected him.

Removing to Chicago, Mr. Miller at once became identified with her largest business interests. His record thus engaged brought him gradually to the political surface, and it was not long before he figured prominently before the people. He always took an active interest in public questions, and was rarely guilty of misconstruing their import. It has invariably been his method to transact public affairs conservatively, on the same basis, in fact, as his private business. This trait in his character, doubtlessly, led to his election to the important position of County Treasurer. Among other positions of political preferment, he has served honorably as member of the County Commissioners, and acted at the time of his recent election as President of that body. He was also, in 1868, a member of the State Legislature.

HERMANN LIEB.

· The People's ticket, in the fall of 1873, elected Hermann Lieb Cook County Clerk, by a very handsome majority.

Mr. Lieb was born in the canton of Turgau, Switzerland, in 1826, and is of Swiss descent on the paternal side. His mother was a Dane. When 19 he left his native place and went to Paris, in France, where he entered a mercantile life in company with his brother. So engaged he remained up to the revolution of 1848. He now entered the Garde Mobile, with which in February and June of 1848 he participated in all of the battles fought during that period in the streets of Paris.

In 1851 Mr. Lieb came to America. A tour through New York, Boston, and Cincinnati preceded his arrival in Illinois in 1856. In this year he settled in Decatur, where he remained until the beginning of the war of the Rebellion. On this event he enlisted in the Eigth Illinois Infantry, under General Oglesby. With this regiment he participated in the battles of Fort McHenry, Fort Donelson, Shiloh, and the siege of Corinth. He was not long in the service — only three months — when he received a Captaincy in Company B. He now accompanied Logan's Division to Vicksburg, where he was placed in charge of the skirmishers. In fact, in the engagements immediately succeeding he performed the same hazardous service. When " The Bend " was attacked he received a painful wound in the left leg. This procured for him a leave of absence. Returning to duty after about a month, Mr. Lieb, under orders from General Grant, raised a colored regiment of heavy artillery, which gained the reputation of being one of the best drilled regiments in the service. Among other recognitions for meritorious service, he was appointed Inspector General of the Department of the Mississippi, and was breveted a Brigadier General.

Having been mustered out, Mr. Lieb went to Springfield and founded the *Illinois Post*, a German Republican paper. After two. years he came to Chicago, and in company with Mr. Brentano, started the *Abend Zeitung*, which took an active part in the polical movement of 1869. A trip to Memphis followed, with a view to establishing a German colony. This movement was a failure, however, owing to the condition of the country. Returning thence, Mr. Lieb established the *German American.* Subsequently he founded *The Union*, a German paper with Democratic sympathies.

M. R. M. WALLACE.

Martin R. M. Wallace, the popular Judge of the Cook County Court, was born in Urbana, Champaign county, Ohio, September 29, 1829, and is consequently in the vicinity of forty-four years of age.

In 1834 his father, John Wallace, removed to Illinois, and settled his family in LaSalle county. In 1839, entering Ogle county, Judge Wallace was placed at school, and, on his removal to Mount Morris, resumed his studies there. At this seat of the well known Rock River Seminary he pursued his academical course. In 1852 Judge Wallace left home, and went to Ottawa. Here he entered the law office of Dickey & Wallace, and remained up to 1856. In this year he came to Chicago, and entered the office of Dent & Black. He also practiced with Major Whitney and Colonel Reading, of Morris.

In 1861 Judge Wallace assisted in raising the Fourth Illinois cavalry, and proceeded to the front as a Major. Having participated, among other engagements, in the battles of Shiloh, Pittsburg Landing, and the movements around Vicksburg, he was mustered out, with the rank of Colonel, in 1864. From this date up to the assumption of his duties as Judge of the County Court, December 6, 1869, he exercised the charge of the United States Assessor's office for the First District of Illinois. In 1873 he was placed on both of the tickets, the "Law and Order." and the "People's," and was re-elected by a tremendous number of votes, Judge of the Cook County Court.

17

JAMES STEWART.

The Recorder of Cook County is James Stewart, a gentleman whose career through life has preëminently been a popular one; affiliating with a class of elements young and vigorous, which rarely fail to advance the interests of their champions.

Mr. Stewart was born in the city of Edinburgh, Scotland, June 24, 1842, and is accordingly thirty-one years of age. Arriving in Chicago at the early age of five years, our subject grew up surrounded by the best influences possible for local success. Educated in the public and High schools, he apprenticed himself to the plumbing business quite early in life, and learned the trade.. He followed it up to about the breaking out of the war, when he joined the Nineteenth Illinois infantry, where he served three years and four months, and where he formed several boon companionships. Mr. Stewart took the Recorder's office, December 21, 1872. From the age of thirteen the Recorder has adopted the motto that "God helps him who helps himself," and has accordingly done so.

AUSTIN J. DOYLE.

The subject of this sketch is Austin J. Doyle, who was elected Clerk of the Criminal Court in 1873, on the People's ticket, by the largest majority given, about 13,000.

Mr. Doyle was the youngest man on the ticket. He was born in Chicago, September 18, 1849, and is, consequently, but twenty-four years of age. His active life, it might be said, was spent amid the duties of the Court the people called upon him to manage. Retiring from school, the first he knew of the world he learned in the dry-goods house of W. M. Ross & Co., where he carried parcels, and was afterwards collector. He then, in 1865, procured a position as clerk in the Recorder's Court, under Hon. Daniel O'Hara, Clerk, and now City Treasurer of Chicago. In 1868, Mr. Doyle was appointed first deputy, *vice* Charles S. Loding who ran against Mr. O'Hara, and was defeated. In 1870, under the new constitution the Recorder's Court was made the Criminal Court of Cook county, Hon. Daniel O'Hara being still the Clerk, with Mr. Doyle, his principal deputy. This position our subject filled when called upon by the popular vote to the very important office he now holds. The secret of Mr. Doyle's success, it may well be said, has been his close attention to business, and his invariable urbanity to everybody.

A man who has prosecuted the duties devolving upon Mr. Doyle, necessarily knows volumes of criminal history. Such knowledge necessarily goes a good distance to make an admirable character reader. This qualification is universally conceded to the subject of this sketch.

JOHN STEPHENS.

The Coroner of Cook county is John Stephens, who has been twice elected by the very largest majorities on his ticket — the first time by about 7,661, and the second time by about 14,000.

Mr. Stephens was born in Albany, N. Y., in 1839, and is of German descent. The family removing to Chicago as early as 1844, or thereabouts, the future Coroner was necessarily placed in a most advantageous situation to grow up with Chicago enterprise and serve in time as one of its prominent exponents. Having spent the rudimental experience of life in the public school and in one of the commercial colleges, Mr. Stephens became employed in the furniture store of Thomas Manahan, of No. 205 Lake street; devoting, like many of his companions, considerable attention to an observation of life as enacted upon the stage. An occasional glimpse in this direction after a time induced him to become an actor himself, in the capacity of property-man, for which his furniture experience peculiarly fitted him. When the war broke out, however, sham battles, in which the vanquished dropped before blank cartridges, lost all charms for Mr. Stephens, and he accordingly entered the 19th Illinois. With this regiment he participated in many hard-fought battles, including about 24 minor engagements. He was always in the front, and was wounded several times. At the battle of Chickamauga, he had his left foot carried away by two grape-shots, and was made a prisoner for fifteen days. While he was created a sergeant, Mr. Stephens yet commanded Company K, at Stone River, and for some time subsequently. When elected Coroner, he was engaged in the Registry Department of the Post-office in Chicago.

Miscellaneous.

PATRICK O'BRIEN.

This gentleman was elected Supervisor for the South Town of Chicago, April 1, 1873, by a majority of over 1,000 — the result of some very active work in the cause of the people.

Mr. O'Brien was born about thirty miles west of the city of Cork, Ireland, January 1, 1830. In 1847 he left his native place, and went to Boston, Massachusetts. Up to 1856 he devoted himself to hotel life throughout various portions of Connecticut and Massachusetts. In this year he came to Chicago, and became identified with the Tremont House, where he remained up to 1860. At this period of his days Mr. O'Brien grew weary of the rush and crush of life in a hotel, and became a street car conductor. After four years of service, he put his accumulations into the liquor business, in which he is at present engaged.

Supervisor O'Brien has figured in the political arena in state, county and city, conspicuously for some time. The most gratifying movement in which he ever was engaged was when, in June, 1872, in company with Messrs. Michael Kelley and McAvoy, he assisted in organizing the Personal Liberty League for the purpose of opposing the obnoxious clause in the State Liquor Law. To this movement he gave all the support he could muster; a fact which is well recognized by the liquor interest everywhere.

MILES KEHOE.

The City Weigher was born in Carlow county, Ireland, August 15, 1845, and arrived in Chicago in 1848, where he was educated in the public schools. Retired from school, Mr. Kehoe pursued general work wherever he could get it, improving himself in his leisure hours as best he could. The result was that, in 1872 he was elected to the Senate — the youngest member that ever sat there. While there, among other bills he introduced the following: The Firemen's Pension Bill; a Bill to Regulate the Election of County Commissioners; and a Bill to Repeal the "Mayor's Bill." He also strenuously opposed the Park Bill, whose defeat saved the West Division the sum of about $700,000. His opposition, especially, to the movement to abolish the Board of Police—being the only man in the Cook county delegation to defend the Board — secured him a great deal of popularity.

During the People's movement, Mr. Kehoe made no less than 38 speeches. He was one of the first to uphold the rights of liquor dealers, under the auspices of the Personal Liberty League.

JULIUS RODBERTUS.

Mr. Rodbertus took a quite active part in the movements preceding the success of the People's Party. He was born in Mecklenburg - Schwerin, Prussia, Sept. 4, 1843. At the age of 13 he left his native place and came directly to Chicago. After a time devoted to various occupations—spending his leisure hours at school — Mr. Rodbertus, in 1859, entered the machine shop of N. S. Bouton, and here learned his trade. He subsequently worked in the shops of the Illinois Central, Galena, and Rock Island Railroads, and in Fuller & Ford's. Finding this employment unremunerative, he afterwards traveled for the *Workingman's Advocate* for two years. While in Bouton's, Mr. Rodbertus joined Company C, of the 19th Illinois, but did not serve therein more than two months; by reason of a severe attack of typhoid fever. When the call was issued for 100 days' troops, he enlisted in Company A, of the 134th Illinois, and served until mustered out.

Politically, Mr. Rodbertus' record dates back to the vicinity of 1863, about which time he was placed on the Third Ward Republican ticket. In 1870, he was elected State and County Assessor for the South Town of Chicago, by a majority of about 25,000. At present he is Assistant Assessor to Edward Phillips, and is also employed in the office of the Collector of South Town. His forte lies in the assessment and collection of taxes.